EVANGELIZATION IN CAMEROON:
Sight and Blindness in God's Revelation in Jesus Christ

BY

REV. MAURICE MEI AKWA

EVANGELIZATION IN CAMEROON:
Sight and Blindness in God's Revelation in Jesus Christ

BY

REV. MAURICE MEI AKWA

EVANGELIZATION IN CAMEROON:
Sight and Blindness in God's Revelation in Jesus Christ

BY

REV. MAURICE MEI AKWA

Maurice Mei Akwa – Christian Evangelization -
Religion and Africa – Gospel of St. John - Catholicism

Copyright © 2016 by Black Academy Press, Inc.

ISBN 0-87831-137-8 978-0-87831-137-8   Paper

BLACK ACADEMYRESS, INC.
4015 OLD COURT ROAD
BALTIMORE, MARYLAND 21208 USA

DEDICATION

To Rev. Robert Leavitt, President/Rector,
St. Mary's Seminary & University
And the Faculty, Staff and Students

This work was
Presented

In candidacy for the degree of

A Licence in Sacred Theology

By

Rev. Father Maurice Mei Akwa

EVANGELIZATION IN CAMEROON:
Sight and Blindness in God's Revelation in Jesus Christ

BY

REV. MAURICE MEI AKWA

ACKNOWLEDGEMENTS

"At times our own light goes out and is rekindled by a spark from another person. Each of us has cause to think with deep gratitude of those who have lighted the flame within us." Albert Schweitzer

Coming to America for further studies was for me and my diocese in Cameroon a rekindling of the light of hope for the formation of future priests for our local church. It was a rekindling of hope because our church is really poor, the poorest among the dioceses of the country. Our young major seminary which depended on religious priests from other countries was soon going to be lacking in formators as the religious priests were reaching the end of their contracts. In fact my bishop did not have money to send priests out on further studies to train for the gradual takeover. It is the scholarship from St. Mary's Seminary & University and the Archdiocese of Baltimore that made it possible for this dream of formation to be realized.

I am therefore grateful to Fr. Robert Leavitt who initiated the scholarship and has paternally done everything possible to make my life here at St. Mary's Seminary & University free of hitches. He has been a real source of inspiration. Thanks also to Fr. Timothy Kulbicki for all the instructions and directives on the life in this community, and for the encouragement he gave for this work to be completed despite the technological strains we went through.

I thank my bishop, Mgr. Roger Pirenne, for allowing me to come for these studies and for his paternal encouragement during the time I spent out of the diocese. I still pledge him my total obedience and accept whatever charge he assigns me on my return to Cameroon.

2

Fr. Paul Zilonka taught me the Gospel of John, and this first contact inspired me to choose John as my working Gospel. He readily agreed to direct my work despite the fact that he was going to be away on sabbatical year. I wish to thank him for his devotion and the patience he exercised while working with me at my slow pace.

I must acknowledge my appreciation for all the wonderful contributions I received from Fr. Michel Tchoumbou, as well as Fr. Jervis Kebei, who sent the valuable material I needed from Cameroon. Both of them have been real brothers and companions in the ministry.

I am also indebted to my sister Hilda Sei Tantoh and my friends Stephen and Veronica Zeh, Ford and True Rowan, Robert Cremen, John Rudy, Bob Dawson, Karen Krukiel and the Christians of the Nativity Parish in Timonium, Lambert Mbom, Mary Elizabeth Tuma, Leonie Mpafe, Boh Herbert, Mike Biboum, Dr. Kenneth and Afu Geh and the Cameroonian Catholic Community in the Washington D.C. Metro-area for their encouragement and the financial, moral and spiritual support they have always given. I also thank Drs. Sebastian and Rose Mezu and their children for their contribution on my research about the church in Africa as well as Tom Chu Meh, Christine Nkwain and Perpetua Ngengwe for proof-reading the final scripts. Thanks to all friends from Weh, Esu and the Menchum Community for making me feel at home in the United States.

This work is dedicated to Fr. Leavitt and the seminary community as a sign of my love and appreciation for all they have been to me. May God bless you and all who have touched my life and been beside me as I prepare to celebrate ten years in the priesthood. I could not list all by name, but I will remember you all in my liturgy of the hours and Eucharistic celebrations

Contents

GENERAL INTRODUCTION

The evangelist[1] who composed the Gospel of John has a specific reason why he wrote a gospel about Jesus. He portrays by signs, which we call miracles, that Jesus is the Son of God. In John 20:30-31, he even emphasizes that the signs in this book are not an exhaustion of what Jesus did, "but these ones are written that you may [come to] believe that Jesus is the Messiah, the Son of God, and that through this belief you may have life in his name." "Come to believe" is an indication that the process that will lead to faith in the Messiah, the Son of God, will be a gradual one. This is necessary for the salvation of those who believe.

The present work is an analysis of a specific theme in this Gospel, sight and blindness, which characterizes the relationship between Jesus and some groups of people we will encounter in the Gospel of John. Inspired by the way our knowledge of scripture was deepened in our study of the Gospel of John, and seeing how much this fitted well with the situation of our local church in Cameroon, we felt we could use this work to contribute our quota to the spreading of the word. We will first briefly look at the message in or behind the Gospel before looking at the background to sight and blindness, as presented in John 9 and 10. We particularly chose this section of John because we saw in it a

---

[1] Raymond E. Brown, *An Introduction to the Gospel of John*, ed. Francis J. Moloney (New York: Doubleday, 2003), 79. While our purpose in this work is not to establish the identity of the writer or author of the Gospel of John, we will at times use John to refer to the writer of the Gospel.

good representation of the situation lived by the Johannine Christians and take this as a turning point of the Gospel. We will use this to illustrate the way the light of the gospel was brought to Africa in general and Cameroon in particular.

As I See it: The Gospel According to John

John sets out to reveal Jesus the word who was in the beginning with God and through whom all that is came to be.[2] He goes on to show that it is a revelation that calls for commitment to the cause of the one who came to save mankind from sin and death. Through comments that clarify certain actions and the sayings of Jesus, the evangelist reveals who Jesus should be to those who see or listen to him. But Jesus himself speaks and through his signs he reveals who he is.[3] Therefore the Gospel of John is a revelation of Jesus by the evangelist and a revelation of Jesus by himself. In 10:37-38, Jesus exhorts the Jews to believe the works he performs, even if they do not believe that he is from the Father, since the works are self-revelatory. "The Jews" are presented in the Gospel of John as opponents of Jesus who are hostile to his teaching and miracles and outrightly reject him.[4] This work is going to bring out a consequence of their rejection of Jesus. After the incident of the cleansing of the temple, the Jews "gradually enter into public conflict (with Jesus, 5:16-18),

---

[2] John 1:1-3.

[3] Sandra M. Schneiders, *Written that You May Believe: Encountering Jesus in the Fourth Gospel.* Revised and Expanded edition (New York: Crossroad, 2003), 48-49.

[4] Brown, *An Introduction to the Gospel of John,* 9.

and a decision is made that Jesus must be slain (5:18). From that point on the Jews are presented as hostile to Jesus and to all who would confess that he is the Christ."[5]

Although it maintains certain common traditions with the Synoptic Gospels, the Gospel of John is unique in its way of seeing and presenting events in the life of Jesus. Jesus visits Jerusalem more than once for various Jewish festivals, where he encounters serious opposition from the Jews long before his death. John presents some authentic historical events. In addition, he interprets them theologically to express the conviction that the Word of God became incarnate in Jesus of Nazareth. John himself testifies that he is an eyewitness.[6] He makes us understand that the signs were performed in the presence of Jesus' disciples, not somewhere in the desert or some remote street. Although his disciples do not understand some of Jesus' actions immediately, they do understand them in retrospect, after his resurrection.[7] Such actions are used to blend the story of Jesus with its theological meaning.[8]

There is an emphasis on experience in the Gospel of John. The issue of knowing Jesus as the eternal word is very important. Jesus even says in his sacerdotal prayer that "this is eternal life, that they should know you, the only true God, and the one whom you sent, Jesus Christ."[9] The Johannine community gazed into

---

[5] 9. Francis J. Moloney, *The Gospel of John*, ed. Daniel J. Harrington, Sacra Pagina, Vol. 4 (Collegeville, Minn.: Liturgical, 1998), 9.

[6] John 19:35; 21:24.
[7] D. Moody Smith, *Johannine Christianity: Essays on its Setting, Sources, and Theology* (Columbia: University of South Carolina, 1984), 216.
[8] 2:13-22. Here the act of cleansing the temple was only understood after the resurrection, indicating that the temple he meant was his body.
[9] John 17:3.

EVANGELIZATION IN CAMEROON: MAURICE MEI AKWA
Sight and Blindness in God's Revelation in Jesus Christ

his glory, the glory he had as the only Son of the Father, full of grace and truth.[10] The revelation, therefore, is a revelation of God the Father in Jesus Christ. When at the end Thomas will demand a sign, touching, in order to believe in the resurrection, Jesus will proclaim as blessed, those who will not see the evidence of his resurrection and, yet, will believe in him.[11] This is an indication that the Gospel of John is also an ongoing experience in the truth about Jesus Christ the Son of God. It is an experience that incorporates Jews and non-Jews. It is a missionary experience that makes the Gospel of John adaptable to all societies.[12]

It is for this reason that the present work also incorporates evangelization in Cameroon as part of the ongoing study of the Gospel of John. This stems from its study of sight and blindness in the revelation of God in Jesus Christ when Jesus stated his mission as sight for those who are blind and blindness for those who claim to see (John 9:39).

Background to Sight and Blindness with Focus on John 9:1-10:21

John 9 presents a man who was blind from birth and who moves towards[13] full sight until he finally encounters Jesus who reveals himself as the Son of Man. At this encounter Jesus says he came for judgment that the blind may see and that those who see may become blind.[14] The encounter with the blind man is also an encounter with the Pharisees who have sent the man out of the

---

[10] John 1:14.

[11] John 20:24-29.

[12] Anthony J. Kelly and Francis J. Moloney, *Experiencing God in the Gospel of John* (New York: Paulist, 2003), 4-5.

[13] He moves towards full sight because we wish to emphasize the fact that it is a progressive movement towards faith.

[14] John 9:39.

synagogue. Jesus in chapter 10 talks to these Pharisees about the shepherd. He speaks so well that, at the end, although some people in the crowd think he is possessed, they are called to order by others who point out that someone who is possessed cannot open the eyes of a man born blind.[15] We therefore take John 9:1-10:21 as a whole because of the link 10:21 makes to the story in chapter 9.[16] We will use the whole in our work on sight and blindness.

Stating the obvious, we would say that sight is seeing and blindness is the absence of sight. In the Gospel of John this theme also exemplifies light and darkness. To have sight is to be in the light and to be blind is to be in darkness. In the present work we will use the story of the man born blind and the miracle of his healing to elaborate on our theme. The blindness of the man from birth is thought by the disciples of Jesus to be caused by sin he committed or the sin of his parents. At the end of the encounter with Jesus, the man comes to sight with faith in the Son of Man, while the Jewish leaders move towards blindness.[17]

Jesus takes the initiative to heal the man, and a conflict arises because of this act. Jesus had used mud made with his saliva to paste on the man's eyes on the Sabbath and made him go and wash. The Jews see this as an act of transgression of the law and indict Jesus as a sinner.[18] For the Jews such a one is not worth knowing and following. Yet Jesus had just said in 8:13 that whoever followed him will not walk in darkness but will have the light of life.

---

[15] John 10:21.
[16] Moloney, *The Gospel of John*, 291.
[17] Moloney, *Signs and Shadows: Reading John 5-12* (Minneapolis: Fortress, 1996), 117.
[18] Martin Asiedu-Peprah, *Johannine Sabbath Conflicts as Juridical Controversy* (Tubingen: Mohr Siebeck, 2001), 197-198.

The conflict among the Jews on the identity of Jesus makes the man who used to be blind see progressively who Jesus is. He comes to light not only in physical sight but also in spiritual sight as he can see clearly that Jesus is a prophet and later worships him as the Son of Man when he sees him with his eyes.[19] The conflict that issued because of the act of Jesus ended in the man who used to be blind being thrown out of the synagogue because of his faith in Jesus.

We wish to show in this work that the act of sending him out of the synagogue proved the blindness of the Pharisees and portrayed them as bad shepherds who do not take care of the weak sheep. This will be in contrast with Jesus, the good shepherd who welcomes the man, makes the man hear his voice, reveals himself to him and lets him become his disciple. If Jesus who is the light is subject to opposition by the Pharisees who are supposed to recognize him but have now become representatives of darkness, then it will be no different for those disciples who will experience the light of life.[20] There is, therefore, a need for good shepherds in the likeness of Jesus for the sheep to be taken care of well.

This is what we have set out to do in the present work. We will show sight as light, as portrayed in the blind man's gaining his sight and seeing clearly by progressively increasing in faith and becoming a disciple. We will also show blindness as darkness, the absence of light. It is the absence of Jesus among those he is supposed to illuminate. We will show the Pharisees as becoming blind from their pride of presuming to know everything about scripture, yet they are unable to perceive the

---

[19] Andreas J. Kostenberger, *Encountering John: The Gospel in Historical, Literary, and Theological Perspective* (Grand Rapids: Baker, 1999), 121.
[20] Andrew T. Lincoln, *Black's New Testament Commentaries: The Gospel According to John*, ed. Morna D. Hooker (Peabody, Mass.: Hendrickson, 2005), 279-280.

hand of God in his Son Jesus. Their expulsion of the man who used to be blind and any other person who professes the name of Jesus, from their synagogues, confirms their spiritual blindness and their failure as shepherds of God's people.

We will, therefore, go on to show good leadership today following the example of the good shepherd as light, and naming bad leadership as darkness. This will come out in the relationship between Jesus, the good shepherd, and present-day church leaders. The formation of present-day church leaders in the seminary as future shepherds of the flock will also be of interest to our work. The case of Cameroon in Africa will show how this concept of leadership in the light of the good shepherd can be applied in the local church with an African experience.

The usage of "the Jews" in the gospel of John in general and in 9:1-10:21 in particular raises questions on the treatment of the Jewish people by Christians. We will therefore make a statement on our understanding of this term before we proceed with our work.

"The Jews" in the Gospel of John

Because of the hostility we find in the Gospel of John between Jesus and "the Jews", we have deemed it necessary to make a statement that clarifies the usage which John makes of them. One could easily mistake the Gospel of John for anti-Jewish if the usage of "the Jews" is not read or taken in the proper context. It is used in a religious-ethnic sense, to describe those who were Jewish and distinguished themselves by their religious practices.[21]

---

[21] Raimo Hakola, *Identity Matters: John, the Jews and Jewishness* (Boston: Brill, 2005), 10-11.

EVANGELIZATION IN CAMEROON: MAURICE MEI AKWA
Sight and Blindness in God's Revelation in Jesus Christ

Although John does not disguise the Jewishness of Jesus he shows Jesus as rejected by his own to whom he was sent (1:11). Throughout the Gospel, the Jewish religious leaders, Pharisees and "the Jews" seem to be interchangeable appellations of the same group. This is because they are the ones who seem to oppose Jesus and his works. Their main contention with Jesus is that he claims to be greater than Abraham (8:51-59) and makes himself God's equal (10:33). They are therefore identified as "the Jewish authorities, not the People of Jerusalem or Judea, still less the Jewish nation as a whole, but simply the men with the power and influence that entitled them to speak on behalf of everybody else."[22] They are the custodians of rabbinic laws and the customs prescribed by the Law of Moses.

In John 9:1-10:21 "the Jews" and Pharisees are used to mean the same group of people. When the neighbors of the man born blind discover he is seeing, they bring him to the Pharisees (9:13) who question him. The questioners are referred to as "the Jews" when they do not believe in the healing act of Jesus (9:18). It is the Pharisees who ask Jesus the question to know if they too were blind (9:40). Yet in the division, after he brilliantly talks to the Pharisees about the good shepherd, is among "the Jews". Pharisees and "the Jews" occur four times each in (9:1-10:21, to confirm that they have equal usage.

A debate is now going on about the relationship between "the Jews" and Jesus as described in the Gospel of John. This goes beyond what actually happened during the lifetime of Jesus. The hostility between the Jews who believed in Jesus and those who did not must have accounted for the way "the Jews" are portrayed. The Christian Jews, in their interaction with pagan converts, undermined some prescriptions of the Law of Moses,

---

[22] John Ashton, *Understanding the Fourth Gospel* (Oxford: Clarendon, 1993), 132.

like in the circumcision of pagan converts, since in the early church Christianity was still regarded as an extension of the Jewish religion (Galatians 4:8). The early Christians were therefore a Jewish group until they started losing their places in the synagogue (John 9:22) due to the hostility against them and their practices. This was also because of their belief in Jesus as their Messiah and King.[23]

The Jewish people as such are not represented in the restricted term "the Jews" and we do not wish to read the Gospel of John as if they were. Many members of the Johannine community were Jews. We therefore refer to "the Jews' in this work, especially in chapters 9:1-10:21 as representing the people who have taken up a theological and Christological position that rejects Jesus and the claims made for him by his followers. Unfortunately, the negative view of "the Jews" has been cause for antagonism and inflammatory rejection of the Jewish people in the history of European Christianity and culture. Christians were involved in or did not quickly oppose the Holocaust which did a lot of evil to the Jewish people.[24]

It is our wish that care will be taken to make sure that writings on the Gospel of John do not make Christianity or at least the Catholic religion sound anti-Jewish. We will take care not to give that impression in the present work.

---

[23] Hakola, *Identity Matters*, 80.
[24] Moloney, *The Gospel of John*, 9-10.

CHAPTER ONE

SIGHT AND/AS LIGHT

John sets out in his prologue already showing Jesus, the Word to whom John the Baptist was witnessing, as "the true light" (1:9) that was "coming into the world" (11:27). He is already showing Jesus as the light of the world that was made through him.[25] Light therefore becomes a major theme in the life and work of Jesus. He will not only declare himself as the light of the world (8:12), but will advise that work should be done while it is still daylight (9:4). This means that the disciples should take advantage of his presence while he is still with them as their light, before the forces of darkness overcome them.[26]

Jesus gives back sight to a man born blind by making clay with his spittle and smearing it on the man's eyes, asking him to go and wash in the pool of Siloam. This was on the Sabbath, a Jewish sacred day of rest and worship (9:6-7). Giving back sight is synonymous with bringing in light to dispel darkness.[27] This act brings a lot of controversy and results in a division among the Pharisees and, after a heated argument, the expulsion from the synagogue of the healed believer in the Son of Man. The Pharisees now intensify their resolve to put Jesus to death since he does not keep the laws of the Sabbath.

---

[25] Moloney, *Belief in the Word. Reading the Fourth Gospel: John 1-4* (Minneapolis: Fortress, 1993), 37.

[26] Moloney, *The Gospel of John: Text and Context* (Boston: Brill Academic Publishers, Inc., 2005), 293.

[27] Craig R. Koester, *Symbolism in the Fourth Gospel: Meaning, Mystery, Community*. Second Edition (Minneapolis: Fortress, 2003), 5.

16

Jesus the Light of the World

When Jesus talks of working while there is still daylight, he is actually referring to his life here on earth. Therefore the Father's will has to be accomplished until he reaches his death that could be compared with the falling of the night. He shows this in various discussions and declarations in chapter 8 when he frees the woman caught in adultery[28], shows his relationship with Abraham, shows who his true disciple is and foretells his death. It was therefore to throw more light on himself, after being accused by the Pharisees, that Jesus declared "I am the Light of the World" (John 8:12) to make his followers aware of who they were following. Light contrasts with darkness, and so those who follow Jesus, the Light, will not be walking any longer in darkness, since the Light of Lights, the light *par excellence*, will be with them. Those who reject the light certainly remain in sin and darkness and are in danger of death and hell, since the Light is also life.[29]

The feast of Tabernacles was drawing to a close, and the last day was characterized by the illumination of the court of the women on the eve of the morning when water was drawn from the spring of Siloam. This is the same water to which Jesus will soon send the man born blind to bathe and be cleansed. It is said that there was so much light in this court, that there was not a court in Jerusalem that was not illumined by the light.[30] If Jesus

---

[28] The Scribes and Pharisees challenge Jesus on what he had to say about who had been caught in adultery but Jesus makes then realize how sinful they themselves are. Instead of condemning the woman he shows that he, the light has come to give life.

[29] Lesslie Newbigin, *The Light has come: An Exposition of the Fourth Gospel* (Grand Rapids: William B. Eerdmans, 1982), 105-106.

[30] Herman Ridderbos, *The Gospel According to John: A Theological Commentary*. Translated by John Vriend (Grand Rapids: William B. Eerdmans, 1997), 291-292.

is therefore the Light of the world, he is that light which illumines all people, the indispensable light that gives life (1:4). He does not only illuminate Jerusalem, but the whole world. Jesus is the one that possesses and dispenses true life. All human searches for true life must culminate in him. Those who become his disciples are not only delivered from the realm and power of darkness, but they also possess the light of life.[31] This is a reaffirmation of a constant refrain in the Gospel of John that the whole reason for Jesus' coming into the world is so that all who believe in him "might have life and have it more abundantly"(10:10).[32] To have life more abundantly means having it to the full because it is through him (1:3-4) that others have life.[33]

Although the prologue of John presents Jesus as the true light that gives light to everyone, the rest of this Gospel shows that not many, especially amongst the religious leaders, are interested in this light. They have chosen to live in darkness and thus have condemned themselves in the fear of being exposed. They are afraid of the light, which is Christ, because their ways of acting are contrary to his way. In his incarnation, therefore, Jesus has brought judgment since he reveals those who are of the light and those who are of the darkness.[34] So long as Jesus is upon the face of the earth, it is day wherever he is since his

---

[31] Jesus is therefore the light of all people of all times. Light is the connotation of many good things: the light of dawn after the darkness of the night; the electric lights which illumine our homes while there is darkness outside; the street lights which shine for everyone and serve as reading spots for students without adequate lighting in their homes; the light that triumphs over the dark forces of ignorance and evil. Christ is all this and more for those who follow him.

[32] Stanley B. Marrow, *The Gospel of John: A Reading* (New York: Paulist, 1995), 125.

[33] Moloney, *The Gospel of John*, 303.

[34] R. Alan Culpepper, *The Gospel and Letters of John* (Nashville: Abingdon, 1998), 136.

EVANGELIZATION IN CAMEROON: MAURICE MEI AKWA
Sight and Blindness in God's Revelation in Jesus Christ

continuous work before his Father serves as a perpetual light to all. That is why he declared in 9:4 that work must be done when it is still day before the night comes and brings with it darkness and fear. This would be experienced at his trial when Simon Peter will be afraid to declare himself a follower of the Man from Galilee (18:25-26).

The idea of working while there is light comes again as caution to his followers when Jesus tells them in John 12:35-36 that the light will be with them only for a little longer. They were therefore to walk while the light was still with them lest darkness overtake them and make them go astray, since the one who walks in darkness does not know where he or she is going. Walking in the light shows the disciples have faith and thus become children of the light, corroborating the prologue of John that showed that to those who accepted the true light, he gave power to become children of God (1:11-13).[35]

Faith in Jesus means faith in God, the one who sent him. Not to accept Jesus is to agree to be overtaken by and to live in darkness, to live in sin. The alternative opening prayer for Ash Wednesday says: "Father in heaven, the light of your truth bestows sight to the darkness of sinful eyes. May this season of repentance bring us the blessing of your forgiveness and the gift of your light." This clearly points to Jesus as light, he who said in John 14:6 that he is the way, the truth and the life. Sin is the opposite of light, and so in the prayer above, sin needs to be forgiven and replaced by the gift of light, sight. To live in the light will mean living in righteousness, while living in darkness means living in sin. True disciples are called to live in truth and not in falsehood, in light and not in darkness.[36]

---

[35] Norman R. Petersen, *The Gospel of John and the Sociology of Light: Language and Characterization in the Fourth Gospel* (Valley Forge, Penn.: Trinity International, 1993), 20.

[36] Brown, *Introduction to the Gospel of John*, 140. Raymond Brown is working here with the Qumran documents and shows that there is a constant

Isaiah 49:6 goes so far as looking at the chosen one, represented by the Servant of Yahweh, as more than a servant. God reassures the servant that he will be a light to the nations so that his salvation may reach the remotest ends of the earth. God the creator will become the hope of the gentiles through his Son. He will go before them and teach by example, the example of love. In this way he will build up confidence in them once more, for their creator, God the Father.[37] The servant is identified as Israel, a collective people to whom God says: "it is too little for you... to be my servant, to raise up the tribes of Jacob, and restore the survivors of Israel" (Isaiah 49:6). This makes them have a personal experience with God.[38] This personal experience gives the people reason to hope again, which is the mission of the light, to bring back hope to God's people.[39] It should be noted that Israel in exile felt the need for God more urgently. Having tasted suffering, they must have experienced hospitality from many, too. Their view of salvation was thus changing so that they saw God as saving them collectively, with his mercy shown also to gentiles and even to outcasts, who will recognize his love, fear his name and agree to keep his word. The treatment of non-Jews and those recognized as outside the law should be more sympathetic as Israel becomes the light that will show God's love and salvation to the world.[40]

---

struggle between the prince of light who is the spirit of truth and the angel of darkness, the spirit of perversion, and all human beings are aligned in two opposing camps dominated by these two powers: the children of light/darkness who walk in light/darkness, and truth/falsehood.

[37] Donald E. Gowan, *The Theology of the Prophetic Books: The Death & Resurrection of Israel* (Louisville: Westminster John Knox, 1989), 157.

[38] Paul D. Hanson, *Isaiah 40-66: Interpretation, A Bible Commentary for Teaching and Preaching* (Louisville: Westminster John Knox, 1995), 130.

[39] Elizabeth Achtemeier, *The Old Testament and the Proclamation of the Gospel* (Philadelphia: Westminster, 1952), 76.

[40] Hyun Chul Paul Kim, *Ambiguity, Tension and Multiplicity in Deutero-Isaiah* (New York: Peter Lang, 2003), 84-85.

The mission of the servant in Isaiah will be fulfilled in Jesus whose humility is exemplary, taking the form of a slave to the point of death.[41] The children of light are bound to become like their master. That is why in the Acts of the Apostles, Paul, the apostle to the gentiles, adapts Isaiah 49:6, to himself and Barnabas, showing that the prophecy was also fulfilled in them as light to the gentiles, conscious of the fact that he is speaking in Christ's name. The light that Christ brought, and is, must shine on all peoples. When Paul personifies the mission of Israel as is found in Isaiah 49:6 many things come into mind in relation to the light. In the Gospel of Luke, at the presentation of Jesus in the temple to fulfill what the Law of Moses prescribed for the first-born children, Simeon proclaimed the 'nunc dimittis.' In it he proclaimed the child as the "light for revelation to the Gentiles, and glory of your people Israel."[42] Simeon goes on to give the qualities of this child, including the fact that he will be cause of the rise and fall of many in Israel, and a sign of contradiction.[43] This effect will be noticed in the reaction of the people after the opening of the eyes of the man born blind in John 9:1-39. Some will be for Jesus and others will be against him because of the same act. Jesus told the disciples after his resurrection in Matthew 28:19, to go make disciples of all nations. It is he who brought the light of the gospel to the gentiles. This also brings to mind the infancy narratives of the birth of Jesus in Luke 2:8-9, when the Jewish shepherds were keeping watch over their flock in the night, and the glory (light) of the Lord shone around them when the angel came to announce the news of great joy.[44]

---

[41] Philippians 2:5-11.
[42] Luke 2:32.
[43] Mark Coleridge, *The Birth of the Lukan Narrative: Narrative as Christology in Luke 1-2* (Sheffield: Sheffield Academic, 1993), 168.
[44] Marcus J. Borg and N.T. Wright, *The Meaning of Jesus: Two Visions* (San Francisco: HarperCollins, 1998), 182-83.

21

Since Israel was to be the light to the nations, to make the presence of the Creator felt, anything contrary to the ways of the Lord was viewed with a lot of mixed feelings. For the Jews, God punished wrongdoing in many ways, even making children suffer the guilt of their parents' sins and vice versa. That is why most conditions that caused pain and suffering were interpreted as punishment for sins committed. This makes us want to see briefly what effects sin had in the Jewish religion, how it influenced the way of living and thinking of the Jews.

Sin and its Consequences in Judaism

Judaism refers to the way of life and the religious practices of the Jewish people following their return from the Babylonian exile in the second temple period. The circumstances brought about by the exile provoked the redrafting of their tradition and brought emphasis more on teaching and ethics than on cult.[45] In the Gospel of John, "the Jews" are referred to as those who oppose Jesus and his followers, though they have many things in common with them like sharing the same scriptures, the same culture, the same language, and religious practices.[46] They are not worse than others who live in sin, but are simply no different, when they were supposed to make a difference. They oppose Jesus and his works although the signs he performs are appealing and point to divine presence in him.

The hostility towards "the Jews" is not directed to them as an ethnic entity but to the religious practices they characterize,[47]

---

[45] F. L. Cross and E. A. Livingstone, *The Oxford Dictionary of the Christian Church* (London: Oxford University Press, 1974), 761.

[46] Mark Allan Powell, *Fortress Introduction to the Gospels* (Minneapolis: Fortress, 1998), 134.

[47] Henk Jan de Jonge, "The Jews in the Gospel of John," in *Anti-Judaism and the Fourth Gospel*, ed. R. Bieringer et al. (Louisville: Westminster John Knox, 2001), 134.

which in the first century consisted in excluding certain categories of people from their synagogues, as was the case of the man born blind, because of their faith in Jesus. This hostility towards them and their practices could also be a move to bring them to reason and make them return to the "right way."[48]

The Jews regarded all that was not according to their laws and custom as sinful. Sin for them had far-reaching consequences, including physical pain and death as punishment from the creator. Francis Moloney points out that even a child born with an ailment was thought to be suffering either because of the sin of its parents, or from sin it committed in the womb.[49] This was because in Jewish tradition both the sinner himself and his descendants had to suffer the consequences of sin. Everything was, therefore, judged from the point of view of sin. This explains why the disciples ask Jesus at the beginning of chapter 9, who sinned for the man to be born blind. Jesus refuses to attribute this blindness to sin despite the fact that illness was thought to be punishment, implying guilt. Jesus goes on to show that the only blindness that would necessarily come from sin will be the blindness of the will.[50]

It is true that sin has a consequence because it stems from disobedience in nature. At creation, God pointed out death to Adam and Eve as a possible punishment if they ate of the tree of the knowledge of good and evil. After the fall, this punishment and the conflict with the devil were extended to their offspring.[51] When David committed adultery with the wife of Uriah,

---

[48] Craig S. Keener, *The Gospel of John: A Commentary.* Volume 1 (Peabody: Hendrickson, 2003), 215.

[49] Francis J. Moloney, *Signs and Shadows: Reading John 5-12* (Minneapolis: Fortress, 1996), 120.

[50] Brown, *The Gospel and Epistles of John: A Concise Commentary* (Collegeville, Minnesota: Liturgical, 1988), 55.

[51] Genesis 2:15-17; 3:15-18.

Bathsheba, and tried to cover up his shame and pride by arranging the death of Uriah, the Prophet Nathan brought David to reason by making him pronounce his own punishment, death. When he came to his senses and realized the gravity of his sin, he pleaded for mercy and God granted him his life but pronounced the death of the child of the adulterous act.[52] And so there were stories circulating about punishments that came from sin. The disciples too might have had these stories in mind when they asked: "Rabbi, who sinned, this man or his parents, that he was born blind?"[53]

For Jesus, "Neither he nor his parents sinned; it is so that the works of God might be made visible through him."(9:3) Although the Jews saw suffering as direct punishment for sin, we are of the opinion that suffering could be a means of proving our faith, or meant for our improvement and edification as shown in other biblical traditions. Take the case of Job the innocent sufferer whom God allowed to suffer, to be chastised by Satan, just to prove to the evil one that there were still righteous ones on earth who were God-fearing.[54] Suffering could also be there to show forth God's glory, making him all in all. In the letter to the Hebrews suffering is shown to be the consolation of believers since they have one who also suffered as high priest and Savior. In fact Hebrews presents a very human Jesus that makes it possible for him to sympathize with other human beings in their weakness and sufferings.[55]

---

[52] 2 Samuel 11 and 12.

[53] John 9:2

[54] James L. Crenshaw, *Old Testament Wisdom: An Introduction* (Louisville: Westminster John Knox, 1998), 92.

[55] Fred B. Craddock, "The Letter to the Hebrews: Introduction, Commentary, and Reflections," in *The New Interpreter's Bible,* ed. Leander E. Keck et al., Vol. 12 (Nashville: Abingdon, 1998), 11.

If our suffering is not a direct punishment for sins committed, then it could be something God allows to happen in our lives for reasons beyond our knowing which nevertheless can help us die to self and find our true life in God. Jesus sees no sin in the man born blind, but others do. The disciples only suggested that it could be the man or his parents (9:2) while the Pharisees are divided over who is the sinner, the man or Jesus who heals on the Sabbath.(9:16) They conclude that the man has been in sin all his life and that Jesus who breaks the Sabbath is also a sinner(9:34).[56]

Sin is a rebellion against God, and it brings disorder to every aspect of human existence. The only way back to the beauty and peace of God's kingdom leads through suffering and pain, manifested by the cross of Jesus, that cross to which the sin of humanity nailed him for the salvation of mankind.[57] We can therefore see from here that sin has far-reaching consequences and is attributed even to very little actions by the Jewish religious leaders. In order to see clearly, we must have Jesus as the healer of sight.

Jesus the Healer of Sight

Although the action of Jesus as the healer is described in just two verses, John 9:6-7, the effects of his action will be or are quite extensive. Jesus the light of the world, who wishes to prove that the works of the one who sent him must be done for all to see in daylight, makes a paste from spittle and clay and rubs it on the blind man's eye and sends him to go wash in the pool of Siloam.

---

[56] David Rensberger, *Johannine Faith and Liberating Community* (Philadelphia: Westminster, 1988), 44.
[57] Bruce J. Malina and Richard L. Rohrbaugh, *Social Science Commentary on the Gospel of John* (Minneapolis: Fortress, 1998), 169-70.

Ironically, Jesus is sent by the Father and he, in turn, sends the blind man to Siloam, which also means "sent."[58] And so, just as Jesus obeyed the father when sent into the world, the man also obeys Jesus when he is sent and gains the sight he had never had from birth. He is now able to see, and his seeing will attract much attention to him and to Jesus. Jesus took the initiative to heal the man. The man did nothing but obey, and came back seeing. Thus the Gospel shows the importance of obedience as a component of faith.[59]

In the Gospel according to Matthew, John the Baptist sends the disciples to question Jesus: "Are you the one who is to come, or should we look for another?"[60] Among other things, Jesus asks the disciples to go tell John that because of him, or through him, the blind regain their sight. Jesus is, therefore, a healer of sight, the one who has come to make the world see clearly what God wants us to do, and so, be free.[61] True freedom, therefore, comes when one is able to see the truth and accept it. Later we will talk about faith as the source of healing. This faith is gained also when one is able to follow the instructions the Lord has given and executes them properly. Many times, in the Synoptic Gospels when he heals those who ask for help he tells them their faith has saved them. Their faith has set them free.

We can see from the miracle of the healing of sight that Jesus is the messiah, the one about whom John the Baptist preached and the one whom the Jews were expecting. It is very ironical that when he came, with all the signs that accompanied his work, those who were expecting him, those who had been prepared by Moses and the prophets, did not recognize and welcome him as noted when the prologue to the Gospel of John said "He came to

---

[58] Ibid., 170.
[59] Paul D. Duke, *Irony in the Fourth Gospel* (Atlanta: John Knox, 1985), 118-19.
[60] Matthew 11:3.
[61] John 8:31-32.

what was his own, but his own people did not accept him" (1:11).[62] From the perspective of the Fourth Evangelist, they could not accept him because their eyes were blinded and so they could not recognize the one they had longed for.

The dialogue between Jesus and Nicodemus in John chapter 3 shows us that to be able to recognize or see Jesus clearly; one needs to be born from above, by water and the Holy Spirit. This is the only means by which believers could be given the grace to be called children of God (John 1:12).[63] Those who did accept Jesus trusted in his word and changed their lives in accordance with his message, and thus became his faithful disciples with their hope for the future secured.

Healing can, at times, be progressive. The healing of the man in John 9 is in two stages; first Jesus puts a substance on his eyes, and then the man is told to go and wash, after which he gains his sight. Jesus is portrayed generally as the healer of the blind in the synoptic Gospels. John shows that Jesus is not just the healer of one person but of the whole world, since he is the light of the world. Coming back to the healing in stages, Mark 8:23 presents another blind person whom Jesus heals. Jesus put spittle in the man's eyes before laying his hands on him, and he started seeing but not clearly. Then Jesus laid his hands on him again and his eyes were totally healed. Jesus makes the blind man in John see the light of day, and then also makes him see the truth of who Jesus is. The truth of who Jesus is happens later, so the healing of the man born blind is even more prolonged than the two stages we see in 9:6-7.

---

[62] Brown, *The Gospel and Epistles of John,* 22-23.
[63] Demetrius R. Dumm, *A Mystical Portrait of Jesus: New Perspectives on John's Gospel* (Collegeville, Minnesota: Liturgical, 2001), 165-166.

Jesus is the Light, but people are divided about him and this is seen in the reaction of the neighbors and the Pharisees to the opening of the eyes of the blind man. First the man says from his ignorance "the man called Jesus" (9:11), and then when questioned by the Jews he says, "He is a Prophet" (9:17) before wondering, "if this man were not from God" (9:33). The climax comes when he accepts Jesus' invitation to believe in "the Son of Man" (9:35, 38).[64] It is this faith in the Son of Man after receiving total sight that provokes the indignation of the blind Pharisees. The blind man had only heard about Jesus, and heard his voice, but now he has met Jesus and seen him with his own eyes, the object of his faith. He looks Jesus in the eye and says, "I do believe," and he worships.[65]

Faith in the Son of Man as Source of Healing and Light

We may be tempted to ask why Jesus had to send the man on such an errand, a blind man who had to walk a distance to wash and be cleansed. Possibly there might be something in the action that contributes to the revealing of God's work that must be done when there is still daylight.[66] The man's obedience is very significant because this is a characteristic of those who wish to be Jesus' true disciples and it has scriptural precedent. In 2 Kings 5:10-14 Naaman the Syrian captain had to obey the command of the prophet to go and wash and be cleansed of his leprosy. Now Jesus sends the blind man to Siloam, which means "sent", to complete his Messianic characteristic,[67] Jesus being the sent one from the Father. In this way the healing and the actions that surround it will point to Jesus as the Messiah, the light that

---

[64] Laurence Bright, *Scripture Discussion Commentary: John* (Chicago: Acta Foundation, 1972), 100.

[65] René Kieffer, *Le Monde Symbolique de Saint Jean.* Lectio Divina 137 (Latour-Maubourg: Cerf, 1989), 61.

[66] John 9:4.

[67] Jesus told his disciples in John 20:21 that "as the Father has sent me, so I send you." His mission is therefore extended to the disciples.

triumphed over darkness. The only thing that can make sense of a dark world, such as the world of the blind man, is the coming of light, a light that does not come from below but from above so that the darkness does not overcome it (John 1:5).[68]

The radical obedience of the blind man therefore is necessary to make him identify himself with Jesus. His obedience is described in just four verbs: he went, he washed, and he came back, seeing. As he responds unquestionably to what Jesus asks him to do, he makes us realize that Jesus is really the living water and the light of the world. When the neighbors will be unable to recognize him, he will boldly say that "I am he" (*ego eimi*) (v. 9),[69] a formula Jesus uses for himself many times in the Gospel of John to describe his mission as light of the world, living water, good shepherd, resurrection and life, and living bread come from Heaven.[70] The blind man entered a new relationship with God, because when an encounter with God takes place, as Isaiah experienced before his call,[71] a transformation takes place. There is a feeling of joy and gratitude as the man looks back at his past life as a beggar. One cannot collaborate with God and the mission of Jesus, or cooperate in its accomplishment, if there is no faith and obedience. "Go and wash in the pool of Siloam" is the order received. With no readiness for God and no faith in his healing power, there will be no reaction.

The blind man is questioned by his neighbors and by the Pharisees (9:10, 15). The Pharisees wish to downplay the healing

---

[68] Newbigin, 120-121.

[69] The usage by the man is not in allusion to the divine name, but as an identification formula. The man identifies himself as the one who was formally blind, while Jesus will say "I am" to identify who he is: light, resurrection and life, way, truth and life, living bread, good shepherd etc.

[70] David Mark Ball, *'I Am' in John's Gospel: Literary Function, Background and Theological Implications* (Sheffield: Sheffield Academic, 1996), 80-81.

[71] Isaiah 6:1-13.

EVANGELIZATION IN CAMEROON: MAURICE MEI AKWA
Sight and Blindness in God's Revelation in Jesus Christ

by calling the man's parents to testify to the fact that he was born blind. There is even intimidation through expulsion from the synagogue of those who profess the name of Jesus, or look upon him as the sent one, a problem that must have been plaguing the Johannine community.[72] The man who used to be blind is honest in all his responses. At every stage of questioning he realizes how much he knows or should know about Jesus. The irony is that just as he progresses in his knowledge and faith in Jesus, the others, the Pharisees, regress. They stick to their religious principles and think Jesus is a violator of their law. They try to obtain the same judgment from the healed blind man who admits to his ignorance of who Jesus really is, but shows them that he cannot be forced into darkness anymore (9:30-33).

It should be noted that when the blind man meets with his neighbors or with the Pharisees, or when the Pharisees question his parents, Jesus is not there. Yet the man bears witness to the little he knows of Jesus. This is an important follow-up to his healing, to be able to bear witness to, and have faith, in the source of his healing.[73] The man is not believed, maybe because of his former handicap. He is insulted as a sinner from birth but he remains firm in the face of all opposition. His faith is strong and advances forward by stages as it does with a catechumen preparing for sacraments. In the end, his eyes are opened to recognize the Son of God outside the House of God, while those who claim to be righteous, continue their activities in the synagogue, blind spiritually. Ellis says that in their blindness, they call Jesus "a sinner".[74] The reward of the man's endurance, obedience, honesty and perseverance is the light of life that we all

---

[72] Charles. H. Talbert, *Reading John: A Literary and Theological Commentary on the Fourth Gospel and the Johannine Epistles* (New York: Crossroad, 1994), 161.

[73] Koester, 63-64.

[74] Peter F. Ellis, *The Genius of John* (Minnesota: The Liturgical, 1984), 164-165.

long to have. It is a reward for his being open to the will of God that brings the fullness of light.[75] We are now set to turn to blindness and darkness and show their effect in unbelief.

---

[75] Leon Morris, *Jesus is the Christ: Studies in the Theology of John* (Michigan: William B. Eerdmans, 1989), 38.

EVANGELIZATION IN CAMEROON: MAURICE MEI AKWA
Sight and Blindness in God's Revelation in Jesus Christ

CHAPTER TWO

BLINDNESS AND/AS DARKNESS

We have tried to show Jesus as the uncreated word according to the prologue of John, the Light of God that came into the world, to lead God's people back to him. He became man and gave human beings, through his teaching and example, the grace and right to be called "children of God." This is because they are begotten by his will. They believe in his name and are baptized. Light is opposed by the darkness of unbelief, represented by those of the chosen race, who refuse to accept or receive the one he has sent. Those who refuse to receive Jesus, the light of the world, those who refuse to believe in him, are identified as the representatives of this world, of darkness.[76] Jesus himself says in John 9:39 that: "I came into this world for judgment, so that those who do not see might see, and those who see might become blind." This is a story that began by showing that physical blindness was not caused by sin, and now closes by pointing out that spiritual blindness, the act of living in darkness, is caused by sin.[77] We will look at some reasons for this persistent darkness.

Obstinacy of the Jews

Reading the Gospel of John from chapters 5 through 10, one will encounter a lot of religious polemic. The Pharisees argue with and denounce Jesus for not abiding by the Law of Moses, or for interpreting it lightly. This could represent a Christian denunciation of Judaism at the time of John, and the Jewish

---

[76] James H. Charlesworth, *John and the Dead Sea Scrolls* (New York: Crossroad, 1990), 18-19.
[77] Brown, *The Gospel and Epistles of John,* 58.

response to this.[78] In the healing of the man born blind, we see him rewarded because of his endurance, obedience, honesty and perseverance in following the light of life we all long to have. But the Pharisees who were blinded by tradition and the "Law of Moses" misinterpreted Jesus, closed up their minds in their pride and could not be enlightened to receive the Light. It is not an example to be emulated.

The miracle of the healing of the man born blind had no precedent. Never in the history of God's people since the creation of the world has a man born blind been given his sight (9:32).[79] Something new and unheard of was happening with the gift of sight to the man born blind. There must be a very special relationship between the person who does such things and God who makes such a new creation possible.

Instead of reading it this way the Pharisees hung on the fact that the making of clay on the Sabbath to impose on the man's eyes was a form of working, doing what was not permitted on the Sabbath, the Lord's sacred day of rest (v. 16). Although this caused a division among the Pharisees, some trying to see God in the healing and others remaining obstinate, it did not deter the Pharisees from condemning the act and trying to minimize the degree of the miracle by asking if the man indeed was born blind, or if the miracle was not a sort of scam. What a costly miracle! They send for the man's parents to testify and the parents also sense that it is not really their son who is being put to the bar but Jesus for whom believers will be expelled from the Jewish places of worship (v. 22).[80]

---

[78] Smith, *New Testament Theology: The Theology of the Gospel of John* (Cambridge: Cambridge University, 1996), 27.
[79] Moloney, *Signs and Shadows,* 127.
[80] Anthony J. Kelly and Francis J. Moloney, *Experiencing God in the Gospel of John,* 207-208.

When the parents do not cooperate, the Jews have no choice but to go to the one who the parents say is old enough to speak for himself (v. 21). The Pharisees tell him to "give God the praise!" but that for their part they know that this man, the healer, is a sinner (v. 24). Their exhortation that he give God the praise is ironic since the man was healed so that the "works of God might be made visible through him" (9:3). Now that this has come to light, he can give praise to God, whose work is not recognized in his servant. We wonder which God is being revealed this Sabbath to be praised since the Pharisees do not recognize him Jesus' works! The blind man asks them if they too want to become his disciples since they ask to know more (v. 27). Knowing more meant wanting to follow as there was a close union between Jesus and his followers.[81] For the once blind-man to make such a suggestion shows that he has become aware of the availability of God's grace even to those who were now judging him. He shows them that God does not listen to sinners, but only listens to the devout who do his will. This is a sign that he believed God had listened to the one who opened his eyes (vv. 30-33).

Although the signs Jesus performs are meant to inspire faith and change believers into living witnesses to the truth in their midst, the Jews remain adamant in their position and, instead, expel the man Jesus healed from their place of worship (v. 34). This is the very fate his parents were afraid of (v. 22). The Pharisees blame his former blindness on his family, telling him that he was born totally in sin (v. 34).[82]

The obstinacy of the Jews shows that it is they who have interpreted the laws to suit their own understanding, according to their ethics. Expelling those who accept Jesus as coming from

---

[81] Gerard Rosse, *The Spirituality of Communion: A New Approach to the Johannine Writings* (New York: New City, 1998), 49-50.
[82] John Wijngaad, *The Gospel of John & Letters* (Wilmington: Michael Glazier, 1986), 84.

God indicates that their misjudgment did not permit them to see far enough beyond their day-to-day interpretation of the Law of Moses.[83] They have sealed their eyes and hearts to reality and have thus become spiritually blind, a state that is worse than the physical blindness of the man born blind. Let us examine the two.

Physical and Spiritual Blindness

To be blind means to lack the power of seeing or to be lacking in perception, sound judgment or logic so as to be insensible.[84] This description suits well with the action of the Pharisees in the story of the healing of the man born blind in particular and the Gospel of John in general. The man born blind was physically blind. He had never seen the light of day and could hardly do anything for himself since he could only distinguish by touch and hearing. He therefore must have resorted, like most blind people of his time, to begging at the entrance to the temple or synagogue, or some popular road junction. It was Jesus' initiative to approach and heal him to give him back his sight, since his blindness was for a purpose, to make God's glory manifest.

Physical blindness is therefore a very serious disability. Bartimaeus in Mark 10:46-52 was a blind beggar who shouted at the top of his voice for Jesus to pity him. From others he had asked for money, but when Jesus asked him what he wanted he answered: "Master, I want to see" (Mk 10:51), a sign that he was desperate for health, and his faith gave him back his sight. He became a disciple of Jesus after the healing and went after

---

[83] Brown, *The Community of the Beloved Disciple: The Life, Loves, and Hates of an Individual Church in the New Testament Times* (New York: Paulist, 1979), 41-43.

[84] Sidney I. Landau, *The New Webster's Concise Dictionary of the English Language: Encyclopedic Edition* (Naples, Florida: Trident Press International, 2003), 76-77.

Jesus.[85] "Son of David, have pity on us"[86] is the cry of two blind men in the Gospel of Matthew, who followed Jesus after the raising of an official's daughter to life. They knew that healing could come from Jesus, already considering him as the Messiah, something their religious officials refused to recognize. They were healed because of their faith, because they believed Jesus could do it; and because of this healing the faith of the crowd was revealed as well, as they could recall that nothing like this had ever happened in the history of Israel (20:30-34).[87]

For the Pharisees, this was the work of the devil. They felt that Jesus was possessed, even when he healed the blind and mute demoniac in Matthew 12:22-24. The Pharisees refuse to see that something mysterious is happening. They try to downplay the importance of Jesus and his acts. This does not, however, take away the fact that Jesus is the Son of God, and he performed a miracle only God could perform. What Jesus declared in John 8:21, that the Pharisees will die in their sins unless they believed that "I Am" (8:24), comes to light in the rejection of Jesus as the Son of Man in chapter 9, with their desire to remain in spiritual blindness.[88]

Jesus performed an incredible miracle in opening the eyes of a man born blind, and it became big news all over Jerusalem. Some of the neighbors of the blind man must have thought that he had a twin running around Jerusalem when they saw him in disbelief and brought him to the Pharisees. The Pharisees claimed that because Jesus did the miracle on the Sabbath he was not from God. They were too strict on Jesus and misinterpreted the context in which he performed the miracle. How could a sinner

---

[85] Bonnie B. Thurston, *Preaching Mark* (Minneapolis: Fortress, 2002), 53.
[86] Matthew 9:33-34.
[87] Donald Senior, *The Gospel of Matthew* (Nashville: Abingdon, 1997), 115.
[88] Mary Margaret Pazdan, *The Son of Man: A Metaphor for Jesus in the Fourth Gospel* (Collegeville: Liturgical, 1991), 45.

EVANGELIZATION IN CAMEROON: MAURICE MEI AKWA
Sight and Blindness in God's Revelation in Jesus Christ

do such miraculous signs? The Pharisees in effect did not deny that Jesus opened the eyes of the man born blind, they understood it well, but instead of asking him if he was indeed the long-awaited Savior, they tried to discredit him. They do not know where he came from.

This is the root of the failure of the Pharisees in the Gospel of John to accept Jesus. They are locked into the former gift of God that came through Moses, and now reject the perfection of God's gift that comes through Jesus Christ.[89] It is a puzzle, too, for the healed man whose eyes and mind are opening progressively. He knows that there must be a link between the fact that someone opened the eyes of a man born blind and his origins. He wonders aloud: "This is what is so amazing, that you do not know where he is from, yet he opened my eyes. We know that God does not listen to sinners, but if one is devout and does his will, he listens to him. It is unheard of that anyone ever opened the eyes of a person born blind. If this man were not from God, he would not be able to do anything."[90] He must have learned his doctrine very well.

This is a challenge to the religious authorities who receive a lesson from a "sinner" fascinated with the "how" of the miracle. In their aggressive affirmation of their superior knowledge, they did not stop to look into the "who" of Jesus. They throw the poor man out of their gathering, accusing him of utter sin (9:34). They throw him out of the religious family, shunning their responsibility of taking care of the weak.[91] Jesus meets the man and confirms his healing by making him profess his faith in the Son of Man. He worships the Son of Man, having seen him with his own eyes, outside the synagogue, prostrating himself in belief

---

[89] 1:17-18.
[90] 9:31-33.
[91] Michael J. Taylor, *A Companion to John: Readings in Johannine Theology (John's Gospel and Epistles)* (New York: Alba House, 1977), 106.

before Jesus, the one who has made God known, the sent one, the light of the world.

We breathe here with relief as Jesus' earlier words to the disciples come true that this man's journey from blindness to sight was "that the works of God might be made manifest in him" (9:3). God's glory is indeed manifested in the man who used to be blind. Jesus reassures him that he came for such judgment: that the blind may see and that those who see may become blind (9:39). The Pharisees who claim they see remain blinded by their sins, because they refuse to see, accept and welcome the Savior of the world, whereas the blind man sees, accepts and worships. Jesus, who heals both physical and spiritual blindness, shows that it is more dangerous to be spiritually blind, because it is sinful.[92] They refuse to see and accept Jesus through his preaching and the signs he works, and refuse to believe in the one God has sent (17:3).

The Pharisees who try to justify themselves and question whether they too are blind are told that: "if you were blind, you would have no sin; but now you are saying, 'We see,' so your sin remains."[93] Those who stubbornly refuse to acknowledge Christ as the revealer of truth are really in bondage of falsehood, thus in sin. The Pharisees took their religion as a guarantee of their status and of vainglory (8:31-33), and so did not come to faith in the Son of God. Jesus does not at all look for status or self-assertion; his whole life and purpose is to reflect the love of the Father.[94] This is what makes him the good shepherd. The Jews, who throw out the healed blind man, show that they are bad shepherds.

---

[92] James McPolin, *John* (Collegeville: Liturgical, 1993), 141.
[93] John 9:40-41.
[94] Bernard Haring, *Free and Faithful in Christ: Moral Theology for Clergy and Laity. Volume 1: General Moral Theology* (New York: Seabury, 1978), 125.

Good and Bad Shepherds as Light and Darkness

The image of the shepherd recalls a favorite theme of Old Testament prophetic literature, as we shall see in Ezekiel and Isaiah. The chosen people are the flock and Yahweh himself is their shepherd. Kings and priests are also described as shepherds or pastors. This could be the reason why Jesus asked Peter in John 21:15-19 to feed his sheep. The sheep belong to Christ, to the sent one, and so he is going to talk in chapter 10 of knowing his sheep and being intimately known by his sheep. This is where the theme of good shepherd comes out, the personal knowledge and treatment of the sheep for which Jesus will be the gate for the sheep and shepherd.[95]

The final encounter between Jesus and the Jews in the presence of the man who used to be blind brings to light the failure of the religious leaders to prove themselves as true custodians of the law, and thus as good shepherds.[96] We know that Jesus is in Jerusalem, under serious threat from the Pharisees, because they feel he is becoming notorious. He is pulling a crowd of sympathizers, of admirers and disciples. We have seen above how he opened the eyes of a man who had never seen the light, and the faith of this man reveals the blindness of the Pharisees. They expel him like a sheep from their flock. He goes to Jesus, the door, and the real shepherd, who does not abandon his sheep.[97]

This is the message of John 10:1-21 which Francis Moloney shows to be a continuation of John 9:39-41. John 9:39-41 is thus a significant bridge to 10:1-21 because of the mention of the blind man's healing in 10:21 which links the story of the good

---

[95] R. Alan Culpepper, *Anatomy of the Fourth Gospel: A Study in Literary Design* (Philadelphia: Fortress, 1983), 109.
[96] Mt. 5:17.
[97] Talbert, 161-162.

shepherd to the story of the man born blind. Jesus has brought life and light to a man born blind who sees physically and spiritually to the detriment of the Pharisees who remain blind because of their obstinacy and are lost in sin and darkness.[98]

The Gospel of John often has a mixture of metaphors that offer different ways of looking at the same reality. The shepherd image in John 10:1-21 will therefore point out Jesus as the gate through which the shepherd will pass into the sheepfold, to bring the sheep to pasture. He will also be the gate by which the sheep will pass out of the sheepfold to green pastures, thus making him the shepherd *par excellence* who knows his sheep even by name and is quite familiar with them. [99] This is the good shepherd, who is ready to be a sacrificial lamb by laying down his life for his sheep (10:11). He will die so that the sheep are saved.

Although there is no suggestion in John that the good shepherd laid down his life to deliver the flock from divine judgment, we see that the shepherd, however, shows his devotion by laying down his life for the flock in contrast to the hired men who care about their own life, and in the face of an obstacle, will disappear (10:12).[100] When the chief priest will send soldiers to arrest Jesus in John 18, they meet Jesus in the garden and he tells them "if you are looking for me, let these men go."[101] He was ready to be taken away while his disciples were freed.

The Pharisees, who wanted to make sure that Jesus was not making a mistake by pointing out that they were blind,

---

[98] Moloney, *The Gospel of John*, 212.
[99] Brown, *Introduction to the New Testament*, 348-349.
[100] Koester, "The Death of Jesus and the Human Condition: Exploring the Theology of John's Gospel," in *Life in Abundance: Studies of John's Gospel in Tribute to Raymond E. Brown*, ed. John R. Donahue (Collegeville: Liturgical, 2005), 149-150.
[101] John 18:8.

coincidentally provoke this discourse, on the good shepherd. They represent the other obstinate Jews who are absent, but discourse could also be directed to those in John's time who were causing division in the community, causing the flock to scatter because they were making themselves rivals of Christ. We must not forget that this encounter is taking place during the feast of Tabernacles and Jesus has proclaimed himself as the living water and the light of the world,[102] key elements of the celebration. When he talks about his relationship to Abraham, that he existed before him, the Jews become hostile and pick up stones to throw at him but he leaves the temple.[103]

Jesus personifies his role as shepherd. He says "I am" and the discussion is dominated by 'I' which appears sixteen times in 10:1-21. No doubt therefore that it is he who offers life, his life, in contrast to the ones that only come to destroy (10:10). He is the one who lays down his life for his sheep, of his own accord, while others fight to preserve theirs; he who knows his sheep and is known by them in the same way as he knows the Father and is known by the Father. Most of the 'I am' sayings are the ones that show us why Jesus is the good shepherd; he acts differently from the others.[104]

The figure of the true shepherd contrasts with the thief, the robber and the stranger who enter the sheepfold by climbing over the wrong way.[105] They enter illegitimately. In the context of John 9:1-10:21, the thief, the robber and stranger could refer to the Pharisees, the Jewish religious leaders, who do not care for the people of God. They seem to have no time for the sick, the handicapped and even those of gentile origin, the other sheep that are not of the fold. Jesus for his part welcomes the weak sheep

---

[102] John 8:12, 9:5.
[103] John 8:59.
[104] Ball, 'I am' in John's Gospel, 96.
[105] John 10:1.

represented by the man born blind who has been thrown out of the synagogue. Smith explains that the Pharisees even evade the wolf by abandoning the sheep.[106] They are sons of darkness and are not working for the total good of the community.

It is easy for us to condemn these Pharisees on the actions and statements they posit in contrast to what Jesus does, but we run the risk of falling into their sin, not seeing our shortcomings and our need for light and forgiveness. That is why we need a shepherd, the good shepherd[107] who will unite the sheep in one fold without discrimination, since he and the sheep will understand each other and be united.[108] The good shepherd is welcoming and even plans to welcome non-Jews, while the Pharisees, the leaders of the people, no longer care for the sheep. To understand what the good shepherd does, let us visit the Old Testament.

The Shepherd Figure in Ezekiel 34

Although there is no direct quotation from the Old Testament in the good shepherd discussion of John 10, we could liken the passage to the biblical tradition of unfaithful leaders of Israel. They are presented as bad shepherds who abandoned their flocks to wolves and caused them to go in exile and live in doubt. God was then presented to them in Ezekiel 34:1-23 as their future shepherd, the good shepherd, who would one day gather his flock

---

[106] Smith, "John," in *The HarperCollins Bible Commentary*, ed. James L. Mays (San Francisco: HarperCollins, 1988), 973.

[107] Leon Morris, *Reflections on the Gospel of John* (Peabody, Massachusetts: Hendrickson, 2000), 367.

[108] Paul N. Anderson, *The Christology of the Fourth Gospel: Its Unity and Disunity in the Light of John 6* (Valley Forge, Pennsylvania: Trinity Press International, 1997), 121.

and make it one.[109] Yahweh was to shepherd his people, Israel, be their protector and grant them abundant life. In Psalm 23:1-4, we meet a precious, caring and generous God whom we liken to the shepherd bringing sheep to green pastures, because of the trust and confidence his care generates in us. With him we are in need of nothing.[110]

But this is not the same with the false shepherds in Ezekiel. Ezekiel addresses the problem of leadership in order to present the transformation that is taking place in Israel. Through the image of the shepherd and his sheep he shows that the Lord intends to reassert divine kingship over Israel.[111] He includes the indictment and judgment on the kings of Israel who exploited their positions to serve themselves, and failed to carry out their responsibilities, which also included the caring for the weak, sick, broken, driven away, lost or vulnerable members of their society. He shows that Israel's kings were ultimately responsible for Israel's demise as they failed to recognize their role as vice-regents of the Lord's flock. The kings fail to care for the sheep. The sheep scatter, fall prey to predators and get lost. Those sheep that were strong enough to survive were ruled with violence.[112]

The consequence of the behavior of the bad shepherds of Israel makes Ezekiel announce that Yahweh will take the flock away from them and that he himself will look after their sheep. This is to say that a unique shepherd will appear descended from

---

[109] Moloney, *The Gospel of John*, 301-03.

[110] Robert Davidson, *The Vitality of Worship: A Commentary on the Book of Psalms* (Edinburgh: Handsel, 1998), 83.

[111] Ezekiel 34:4-5.

[112] Ralph W. Klein, *Ezekiel: The Prophet and his Message* (Columbia: University of South Carolina, 1988), 121-122.

EVANGELIZATION IN CAMEROON: MAURICE MEI AKWA
Sight and Blindness in God's Revelation in Jesus Christ

David, who will feed, protect, save and gather the lost sheep.[113] In John 10, Jesus presents himself as this shepherd who looks after his sheep, seeks out the strayed, cures the crippled ones and carries the weak on his shoulders. He brings them into the fold so that there will be one flock and one shepherd.

Although Jesus' message is first of all to the lost sheep of the house of Israel[114] his message extends to everyone, fulfilling the ancient promise that the Messiah's rule will cover the whole world (Isaiah 2:2-6; 66:18). This is a proof of Christ's love for his people, as exemplified in the concern he shows to the man born blind. But it was not the same with the Pharisees in John 9-10. They did not show concern for the people, especially the vulnerable ones. All their emphasis was on the law.

Expulsion from the Synagogue because of Jesus [115]

What we are actually witnessing is a division among the Pharisees that was caused by the sign Jesus accomplished on the man born blind (9:16). His healing of the man born blind did not lead to the praise of God for his wonders among men, but to division. The Pharisees are not sure that this man in front of them was born blind. So they call his parents to testify since having known him from birth their evidence would be more credible. The parents of the man were afraid of the Jews who had decided that anyone who confessed Jesus as the Christ was to be cast out

---

[113] Margaret S. Odell and John T. Strong, *The Book of Ezekiel, Theological and Anthropological Perspectives* (Atlanta: Society of Biblical Literature, 2000), 54.

[114] Matthew 15:24.

[115] We are using the expulsion of the man born blind and others from the synagogue (9:34) as an example of bad shepherding.

of the synagogue. In other words, they were to be excommunicated. (9:22).[116]

The parents of the man born blind might not have been the only people who did not wish to be involved in a debate about the status of Jesus, no matter how convinced they were of his divine origin. John 12:42 speaks of many authorities who believed in Jesus, but for fear "of the Pharisees they did not acknowledge it openly in order not to be expelled from the synagogue." The situation must have been very tense because of Jesus that even these Jewish leaders were afraid to publicly recognize him. They did not want to face being excommunicated by their colleagues or compromise their social positions.[117]

The agreement by the Jews to expel believers from the synagogue as 9:22 shows us was a way of separating those who confess that Jesus is the awaited Messiah and those who did not. This is how the verse reads: "…for the Jews had already agreed that if anyone acknowledged him as the Messiah, he would be expelled from the synagogue." This shows that a meeting had taken place because of Jesus to show that it was not compatible to be a disciple of Jesus and a disciple of Moses at the same time (9:28-29). So their membership in the synagogue had to be discontinued.[118]

The blind man was therefore expelled from the synagogue when he showed them that he was a disciple of Jesus: "Do you want to become his disciple too?"[119] They did not want to be

---

[116] Albert Kirk and Robert E. Obach, *A Commentary on the Gospel of John* (New York: Paulist, 1981), 133.

[117] Andrew T. Lincoln, *The Gospel According to Saint John* (New York: Continuum, 2005), 358-359.

[118] J. Louis Martyn, *History and Theology in the Fourth Gospel*. Third Edition (Louisville: Westminster John Knox, 2003), 46-47.

[119] John 9:27.

45

enlightened by the one who had already received the light of Christ, because as bad shepherds, they were close-minded. Though their minds were made up and they wanted the healed man to say what they wanted him to say, he remained clear and determined in his line of thought.[120] The man who was born blind therefore demonstrates a lot of courage, but what of his parents?

Fear of the Parents of the Blind Man

The parents of the blind man are extremely cautious. They are able to testify to the fact that this was indeed their son and that he was born blind (9:20-21). This confirmation now makes it clear to the Jews that the miracle has taken place. But the parents were afraid of the Jews, afraid of losing their place and status in the synagogue. They were afraid to debate with the Jews under the tense atmosphere and so declare ignorance of the source of his healing.[121]

The parents of the man born blind could not even praise and thank God publicly for the wonders that had occurred to their son and so be drawn into the mystery of Christ, the miracle worker. Certainly their agony might have been great, given the guilt over the possibility that it was their sin that was responsible for their son's blindness. In such a situation the healing was also extended to them.

Instead of bearing witness, though they might not have been there when Jesus healed their son, they send their interrogators back to their son, who is an adult and could speak for himself.

---

[120] Robert Kysar, *John's Story of Jesus* (Philadelphia: Fortress, 1984), 50.
[121] Ernst Haenchen, *John 2: A Commentary on the Gospel of John Chapters 7-21* (Philadelphia: Fortress, 1984), 39.

Their fear overshadows their joy.[122] They leave their son at the mercy of these angry Pharisees, like a bad shepherd who abandons the sheep when in danger of a wolf. This could also be an indication of the type of family divisions that occurred when fear made family members turn their backs on others because of Christ or for fear of being thrown out of the synagogues. Raymond Brown says that the parents of the man born blind and others who were afraid of publicly identifying with Jesus, valued human respect over God's glory.[123] They had not yet come to the light.

Let's revisit John 9:39 and see the purpose once more of Jesus' coming, which will permit us to go ahead with our line of reasoning.

IV. John 9:39 Revisited

The formerly blind man has completed his healing. His eyes and heart are open, and he can see daylight as well as see clearly the source of his light. After his expulsion from the synagogue, he meets Jesus outside who asks him if he believes in the Son of Man. His question is: "Who is he, sir?" And when Jesus points out that it is Jesus, the one standing in front of him, the man progresses to address Jesus as "Lord" already expressing deep faith in the Son of Man, the Messiah. This is when Jesus seems to sigh with relief and show that "I came into the world for judgment, so that those who do not see might see, and those who do see might become blind."[124]

---

[122] Jean Vanier, *Drawn into the Mystery of Jesus Through the Gospel of John* (New York: Paulist, 2004), 175.
[123] Brown, *An Introduction to the Gospel of John,* 76.
[124] John 9:39.

His coming into the world and to the man born blind, as light, is also the moment for decisions and for judgment. We have seen the man born blind go through stages of healing to become a disciple of Jesus. The action of Jesus' opponents has also progressed from just debate and division to judgment and final expulsion of the disciple from the spiritual gathering. Jesus' revelation of his mission on earth makes us understand the previous points better.

Jesus came for judgment, and his judgment both enlightens and blinds.[125] He did not come to judge and condemn at this stage. Such condemnation takes place when the light reveals that which is in darkness and exposes the deeds of men. In it individuals' relationships with God are brought into the open. Jesus is using the healing of physical blindness to speak of the spiritual condition of the Pharisees.

A curious crowd must have gathered around the formerly blind man who now proclaims his faith in Jesus. This shows that some believe in Jesus and have sight, while others reject him and become blind. According to McPolin, the Pharisees are those who see according to the Law of Moses and boast about it. They have become blind, incapable of comprehending what Jesus has brought. On the other hand, the man who was blind is not proud, he knows he is ignorant and lets himself be touched by Jesus and comes to light.[126]

The revelation of God in Jesus Christ therefore brings light that exposes the religious authorities and their inadequate judgment. Condemned as blind, they will be shown to be thieves and robbers, strangers and hirelings. They, who thought they alone, had access to the light and could decide who is and is not a

---

[125] John Ashton, *Understanding the Fourth Gospel* (Oxford: Clarendon, 1993), 232.
[126] McPolin, *John*, 141.

sinner, and prosecuted those who dared to challenge them, have now been proven wrong.[127] Some smart guys in the crowd in v. 40 do realize an intrigue in what Jesus seems to say to the healed friend, although he was actually talking to those watching and listening. They ask a question to be sure of what their ears had heard. Jesus had rejected the fact that being disabled physically was the consequence of sin. Now he shows that it is guilt that incapacitates, the guilt that comes from the willful turning away from the light that reveals the presence of the sent one.[128]

Their encounter with Jesus provokes a discussion on good leadership, the good shepherd whose link with the story of the man born blind culminates in 10:19-21 where it is confirmed that the one who opens the eyes of a man born blind could not be possessed. This paves the way for our looking at sight and blindness in leadership.

---

[127] Dorothy Lee, *Flesh and Glory: Symbol, Gender and Theology in the Gospel of John* (New York: Crossroad, 2002), 98.

[128] Michael Dauphinais and Matthew Levering, *Reading John with St. Thomas Aquinas: Theological Exegesis and Speculative Theology* (Washington, D.C.: Catholic University of America, 2005), 136.

49

CHAPTER THREE

SIGHT AND BLINDNESS IN LEADERSHIP

To have sight is to be able to see. This sounds obvious. Yet it is often dangerous when someone who sees physically is said to be blind. This means that the person lacks perception, and maybe a spirit of right judgment and distinction. Having sound sight and not being blind are important characteristics in leadership. This can be understood in the description of the good shepherd and the relationship he has with his sheep.

It had been foretold in the prophet Ezekiel that a day would come when God would gather together the dispersed sheep of his people, Israel, so that they would live in their land once more.[129] For the Jews, in the time of Jesus, this meant that the shepherd would revive and restore their former prosperity. They were once more going to be a privileged nation among other nations. The Jewish leaders had failed to behave as true pastors of the people of Israel.[130] Because of their failure Israel suffered many ills in the hands of foreign kingdoms. Even now in the time of Jesus the religious leadership of the people of God is not exemplary.

Jesus now reveals the real blindness of the Jewish religious leaders in John 10, since they do not see the spiritual needs of those they are meant to shepherd, but lay emphasis on the observance of the law. Although they are legalistic they fail to apply the law to context.[131] The leadership Jesus proposes is one of total union with his sheep; he knows them and they know him. It is a protective leadership in which Jesus, the shepherd, lays

---

[129] Ezekiel 34:27-28.
[130] Mark W. G. Stibbe, *John's Gospel* (New York: Routledge, 1994), 24.
[131] Ibid., 80.

down his life for the safety of the sheep. Jesus, therefore, is the way into and out of the sheepfold, and thus the way to heaven.

We are now going to look at sight and blindness in leadership, taking cognizance of the fact that the leadership Jesus proposes here is one of guidance. It is the leadership in which the shepherd knows himself and has a well-communicated vision that enables him to build trust and confidence among those that are led.[132] He takes effective action to realize his own potential and, thus, positively influences the behavior of those who are led. He does everything to promote self-respect and freedom since Christ compelled no one to follow him. His sheep were influenced by the voice they recognized. The man born blind clung to the truth of the shepherd whom he had seen and touched and of whose goodness he had tasted.[133] The life of the shepherd/leader allows for reflection and even contemplation since his labor is quite intensive and, at times, risky. We will therefore look at the good shepherd and/in some leaders and their various situations.

The Good Shepherd and Jewish Leaders

It was the Jewish leaders who sent the man who used to be blind out of their synagogue because of his sympathy with Jesus. The Jews were governed by Torah principles[134] guided by prophets, priests and heads of the various tribes of Israel. Their leaders had the duty to make God's law known to them and guide them through the observance of this law. The teachings were given often in the synagogues, in the temple and at home. In the Gospel of John, the leaders are simply referred to as Pharisees.

---

[132] Peter M. J. Stravinskas, *Our Sunday Visitor's Catholic Encyclopedia* (Huntington: Sunday Visitor, 1991), 281.

[133] Scott Gambrill Sinclair, *The Road and the Truth: The Editing of John's Gospel* (Vallejo: BIBAL, 1994), 50.

[134] These were the principles of the Law as laid down by Moses in the Pentateuch. To these the Pharisees added the Jewish written and oral law which determined their religious practices.

51

Their main concern was to fulfill all God's ordinances in the Torah, and as spelled out in the tradition of the scribal elders. This tradition laid heavy emphasis on ritual purity and boundary keeping.[135]

Purity meant that the Jewish people had to keep away from that which could result in uncleanness. Thus they kept away from persons with certain disabilities, lepers, public sinners like tax collectors and prostitutes, as well as from non-Jews. It all boils down to the scribal interpretation of Torah directives in no mixture, that is, of persons, foods and clothing materials. This law was to be observed at all times with no distinction of persons in all Jewish communities. Jews were to be ritually pure.[136] They had to be holy as the Lord their God is holy in order to remain pure. When that which is holy was mishandled, especially by an outsider, they felt it was profaned, polluted and defiled. God and human beings were known to have exclusive persons, places, objects, times and places that had to be respected by others. That is why the Pharisees distanced themselves from those individuals who showed an indifference to the law or interpreted the purity rules lightly.

The man born blind was thus thought to be a sinner because of the disability that was taken to be a sign of sinful or impure birth.[137] The idea of purity had grown so strong that sin was interpreted in anything the Pharisees found irregular. Much of their judgment never took circumstances into consideration and so could be applied out of context. Jesus has taken the initiative to heal the man born blind, and so make God's glory manifested. Instead of praising God for such powers on earth, the Pharisees declared Jesus a sinner because he made mud to paste on the eyes

---

[135] Malina, *Social Science Commentary*, 177.
[136] Ibid., 177. Ritual purity meant keeping away from contamination.
[137] Haenchen, *John 2*, 40.

on a Sabbath day. Making mud with his saliva was considered as working. For the Jewish religious leaders, Jesus' origins cannot be from God and because the blind man had been a sinner from birth, he can only associate with Jesus, another sinner as himself. This was actually being blind to reality.[138]

Logically, if the Jewish leaders considered themselves protectors of the children of God, they would have acted like the shepherds that protect sheep. They would have advised the man born blind on those with whom he could associate and those with whom he could not. Instead they cast him out of the community, abandoning him to the mercy of the one they said was not from God. They sent him to the stranger and thus failed in their duty as shepherds of the flock.

The shepherd, according to Isaiah, feeds the flock, gathers and protects the lambs, and looks after them with care.[139] When danger comes, the shepherd bravely faces it for the safety of the sheep. This is what David confessed to Saul that he did when he convinced Saul that he was capable of fighting with and killing the giant of the Philistines. He told Saul, "Your servant used to tend his father's sheep, and whenever a lion or bear came to carry off a sheep from the flock, I would go after it and rescue the prey from its mouth. If it attacked me, I would seize it by the jaw, strike it, and kill it."[140] This is what the Pharisees failed to do when they dismissed the healed man as a man born in sin, and threatened to excommunicate anyone who sympathized with Jesus.[141] This action of the Pharisees makes us conclude that they were not true shepherds.

---

[138] Fernando F. Segovia, *"What is John?" Readers and Readings of the Fourth Gospel* (Atlanta: Scholars, 1996), 74.
[139] Isaiah 40:11.
[140] 1 Samuel 17:34-35.
[141] Mark A. Matson, *John* (Louisville: Westminster John Knox, 2002), 59-60.

It is not easy to be a true shepherd, knowing the duties that go with it.[142] The shepherd is often away from home because he has to look after the sheep even at times in the night. He is out in the cold and other changing weather conditions. He eats irregularly and has to make sure that the sheep are well protected. Alone, the sheep is a particularly harmless and helpless animal, and its care needs to be very intensive. The sheep need to flock together. They are not as aggressive as the goat and from experience we have noticed that they do not usually fight in self-defense or resist any intruder the way the goat will. The sheep needs time to know how to look for foliage, water or, in short, fend for itself.

In a flock, when one sheep goes in a certain direction, it is possible for the others to go the same way. It is because the shepherd spends so much time with his sheep that he has to be recognized and followed by them. They will certainly flee from the stranger who will not know how to treat them the way the shepherd treats them. It is not easy for an intruder to usurp the shepherd's role. If he does, the intruder puts the life of the sheep in danger.[143]

The Pharisees in John 9, the supposed religious shepherds of God's people, regarded Jesus as an intruder saying that he does not come from God. Yet they did not do enough to prevent him from misleading those they were supposed to protect from wild wolves. The poor harmless man who was born blind is in danger in their hands as they brutally send him out of their flock. The true shepherd takes him back into the sheepfold. It is Jesus who recognizes the man, the same Jesus who had taken the initiative to heal him. Jesus welcomes the man because he knows his

---

[142] Ibid., 66.
[143] Helen C. Orchard, *Courting Betrayal: Jesus as Victim in the Gospel of John* (Sheffield: Sheffield Academic Press, 1998), 139.

sheep, contrary to false teachers who were usurping the place of God's messengers.[144]

Jesus is the true shepherd and he himself describes the characteristics of a true shepherd. He is the one that enters the sheep pen by the door. The doorkeeper allows him to enter because he is known. The sheep hear the voice of the shepherd and respond to him (10:2-4). Although there are many sheep in the fold belonging to various shepherds, only the ones which recognize the shepherd's voice will go out and follow him, as the man who used to be blind heard the voice of Jesus the true shepherd and became his disciple.[145] The true shepherd does not drive the sheep. He leads them (10:4).

The false shepherd, on the contrary, does not enter the sheep pen through the gate. This is because the doorkeeper does not know him and will not allow him access. The false shepherd is indeed a thief and robber (10:1). This is the description Jesus uses of the false teachers that came before him. The Pharisees did not measure up to the qualities of the true shepherd and failed to see this and improve when Jesus brought them the light. So they remain in darkness. They refuse to have anything to do with whatever Jesus says or represents. They remain glued to the Law of Moses and the traditions of the law Christ is fulfilling.[146]

Jesus shows that as a true shepherd, he came to the sheep pen of Judaism by the right channel. He seeks out those who are his, and calls them by name and leads them to righteousness. It is in the story of the man born blind that we explicitly find the

---

[144] Sandra M. Schneiders, *Written that You may Believe: Encountering Jesus in the Fourth Gospel* (New York: Crossroad, 2003), 77.
[145] John Ashton, *Studying John: Approaches to the Fourth Gospel* (Oxford: Clarendon, 1994), 126-127.
[146] Sharon H. Ringe, *Wisdom's Friends: Community and Christology in the Fourth Gospel* (Louisville: Westminster John Knox, 1999), 56.

fulfillment of the qualities of the good and bad shepherds. The hearing of the voice of the good shepherd is demonstrated in the healed man's clinging to Jesus and his persistent refusal to pay attention to the voice of the Jewish leaders who did not recognize the hand of God in his healing. Jesus is the shepherd for the sheep that have no shepherd, for the sheep that strayed, and for the sheep that are exploited.[147]

Jesus is the good shepherd who has asked his disciples to do as he did. We will now turn towards the Christian church leaders and see their relationship with the good shepherd.

Jesus the Good Shepherd and Church Leaders

Jesus remains the true shepherd of the sheep. He will tell Peter in John 21 to take care of his sheep. Therefore, it is he who provides access to the fold, which has become his church, and all must pass by him to the Father.[148] The Jewish leaders placed over God's people, as shepherds, did not take good care of them and have been exposed as blind. Jesus shows that he is the good shepherd by what he does for the neglected people of God. He shows that church leaders, beginning from Peter, must serve willingly, guarding the flock from wolves, false teachers and false messiahs. It is they that lead the flock to good pasture and make sure that they are well fed, since Christ himself is the bread of life. They will not control the sheep by barking orders at them, but by leading them through familiar relationships, making sure that none is discriminated against.[149] In this way they will know the sheep well and will be known and understood by the sheep.

---

[147] Ridderbos, 353.

[148] Chi Rho, *Commentary on the Gospel According to John* (Adelaide: Lutheran Publishing House, 1988), 185.

[149] Smith, *John Among the Gospels*, Second Edition (Columbia: University of South Carolina, 2001), 227.

There is a problem when church leaders act as if they were the good shepherd and not his vicars. Even church leaders must depend on the good shepherd for guidance and protection without fear of abandonment.[150]

There is an interesting note on leadership in the First Letter of Peter where the author exhorts the presbyters (elders) as an elder himself and a witness to the one who lay down his life for his sheep. He tells them to "Tend the flock of God in your midst, [overseeing] not by constraint but willingly, as God would have it, not for shameful profit but eagerly. Do not lord it over those assigned to you, but be examples to the flock. And when the chief shepherd is revealed, you will receive the unfailing crown of glory."[151] The author of First Peter is putting forth the shepherding of the flock by church leaders as the will of God. The important thing for them to do is to care and lead freely, striving to teach by example. There will be an eternal reward for those who remain faithful since the chief shepherd will come back to take stock. The fundamental reminder to the leaders is that the flock is God's flock and they are only caretakers and not masters.[152]

Jesus does not want the conflict that characterized his relationship with the Pharisees to contaminate the work of his disciples and their successors. So he encouraged them to take courage in all their troubles, since he had overcome the world (16:33). They were to do everything to make sure that the flock was well taken care of. Jesus himself set the pattern for how church leaders would function. He was selfless in his service

---

[150] Ronald W. Richardson, *Creating a Healthier Church: Family Systems Theory, Leadership, and Congregational Life* (Minneapolis: Fortress, 1996), 74-75.
[151] 1 Peter 5:1-3.
[152] David L. Bartlett, "The First Letter of Peter," in *The New Interpreter's Bible*, Vol. 12, 314-315.

without seeking to gain applause or stature. The Jews belittled him, but he never sought to justify his status outside the work he did. He told them that if they did not believe in what he said, they were to believe in his works, since he did his Father's will.[153] Church leaders are, therefore, called upon not to do their will but the will of the supreme shepherd, whose servants they are called to be.

Corrupt leaders and false shepherds exist. They gave God a bad name in Israel's past and are trying to tarnish the image of the church now as well. These are those that behave as hirelings. The sheep do not belong to them. They are not ready to risk their lives or honor for the cause of others and do not prepare the sheep for eternal salvation.[154] Bad shepherding is never acceptable in the church.

Jesus qualified as a good shepherd not merely by revealing the Father whom he fully knew, but also by giving his life for the sheep.[155] Jesus will tell the disciples in John 15:13 that love also consists in laying down one's life for one's friends. Although Jesus lays down his life in obedience to the Father's will in order to take it back again in the resurrection, suffering and death have become aspects of the life of the leaders of the church and other Christians. If the sheep are to have life in abundance, the shepherd must be ready to offer his life for them.

The willingness to risk one's life for the sheep, putting oneself in the way of danger so that the sheep are safe, is a unifying and reassuring factor for the sheep that are thus protected. After all, when there is no leadership, or the leadership is incompetent, the sheep scatter. Without leadership the sheep become confused and each turns and goes its own way. If the

---

[153] John 10:38.
[154] Reginald Garrigou-Lagrange, *The Priest in Union with Christ* (Rockford: Tan Books, 2002), 163.
[155] Chi Rho, 182.

shepherd is a hired outsider, he will also likely flee at the approach of danger. The prophet Zechariah foretold that when the shepherd is struck, the sheep scatter.[156] Pope John Paul II warns that it is not good at all for church leaders to deserve the name of "hireling", the name of the one to whom the sheep do not belong, the one who abandons the sheep and runs away in danger, because the sheep do not belong to him. He adds that the solicitude of every good shepherd is that all people may have life and have it to the full, so that none of them is lost, but have eternal life.[157]

With God himself as the chief shepherd and the leaders of the church as co-shepherds, the mission of shepherding becomes a fragile one because of the weakness of the human shepherds. When a shepherd recognizes this limitation in his office and relies on God, he is bound to succeed.[158] As God has entrusted the Pope and Bishops with the task of shepherding the church, so too have they shared their ministry with priests. This sharing of power does not diminish the authority of the shepherds, but permits them to be more efficient and successful.[159] The community then benefits from his hospitality and that of God, who leads the church as he led the flock of Joseph.[160]

It is therefore imperative that the leaders of the church be devoted to their mission for the salvation of the souls of the sheep God has entrusted to them through his son. Jesus has other sheep that are not in the fold and that must be brought into the fold also

---

[156] Zechariah 13:17.
[157] John Paul II, *Letters to my Brother Priests, 1979-2001.* John Socias, Editor (Princeton: Scepter, 2001), 13-14.
[158] Brendan Byrne, *The Hospitality of God: A Reading of Luke's Gospel* (Collegeville: The Liturgical, 2000), 58.
[159] Robert H. Welch, *Church Administration: Creating Efficiency for Effective Ministry* (Nashville: Broadman & Holman, 2005), 71.
[160] Psalm 80:1.

EVANGELIZATION IN CAMEROON: MAURICE MEI AKWA
Sight and Blindness in God's Revelation in Jesus Christ

(10:16). This indicates urgency in the work of the leaders of the church to work towards bringing the whole world into the fold so that other sheep may belong formally to the fold. It is then that the teaching on "one flock and one shepherd" will have meaning, when the Holy Father becomes the Supreme Pontiff of all Christians. Although this is a long way from what it meant in John's Gospel, only in this way will God's people live in confidence, contented and flourishing in the best of life.[161] We will now look at the importance of good shepherding in the formation of future Church leaders.

Jesus the Good Shepherd and Seminary Formation

The healing of the man born blind was provoked by the question the disciples asked Jesus, to know more about the association of sin and suffering. They must have been curious and wanted to learn more from Jesus. The Gospel of Mark also presents Jesus as calling his disciples to be with him first of all, so that he might send them out on mission.[162] They had to learn from the master what the exigencies of their ministry were. In the Gospel of John, the training is gradual and the understanding is progressive. The man born blind, because of the light he had received, progressively discovered the various attributes of Jesus until he finally proclaimed him Lord. He found in Jesus the gate to the sheepfold where all are brothers and sisters. Martha told Jesus: "I have come to believe that you are the Messiah, the Son of God..."[163] when Jesus told her that he was the resurrection and the life.

---

[161] Richard R. Gaillardetz, *By What Authority? A Primer on Scripture, the Magisterium, and the Sense of the Faithful* (Collegeville: Liturgical, 2003), 59.
[162] Mark 3:13-19.
[163] John 11:27 Coming to believe indicates that the events in the life of Jesus have gradually influenced Martha that he is the Messiah.

The seminary is a nursery for the formation of future priests. It is a time of learning from and about the shepherd, to know his ways and thus be ready for the task of shepherding. We live in a world in which there is little regard for moral values anymore. That is why the ministry of the priest needs to be exercised by capable co-workers in the gospel of Jesus. The interaction with the Pharisees in the story of the man born blind and the parable of the good shepherd reveal the necessity for solid training. No doubt the Second Vatican Council stressed that "The whole training of the students should have as its objective to make them true shepherds of souls after the example of our Lord Jesus Christ, teacher, priest and shepherd."[164] As teacher, "Christ teaches in all our striving, don't lose sight of the real purpose – it is not about us, our position, or our authority, but about God's work and the needs of others."[165]

Just as "the Jews" in John were reluctant to open up to the light that Jesus the true shepherd was bringing, so too do some members of the flock today resist what could be termed the progress of the world. Globalization is making the world a village and seminary training must be done in consideration of the various aspects of development, how pastors can fit in to the challenges of our days.[166] The prophetic message should be given in such a way that all would feel and act like members of the fold and not act like strangers.

The guidance of the Spirit is needed in this so that the pastor will be able to collaborate with those working to make the

---

[164] Documents of Vatican II, *Optatam Totius*, 4

[165] This is part of Fr. Leavitt, President/Rector of St. Mary's Seminary and University's sermon during the Alumni Day Mass of October 16, 2006.

[166] Richard A. McCormick, *The Critical Calling: Reflections on Moral Dilemmas since Vatican II* (Washington, D.C.: Georgetown University, 1989), 128.

EVANGELIZATION IN CAMEROON: MAURICE MEI AKWA
Sight and Blindness in God's Revelation in Jesus Christ

community life easier to bear with.[167] The man born blind was able to make comments about Jesus and his identity through the questions that the neighbors and the Pharisees, themselves, asked him. The future priest should also be attentive to the fact that there will be groups of people who will either help him to achieve his mission or fail in it. There will be teams of trained and reliable laypeople around the priest as collaborators, given the reduction in candidates for formation from most dioceses. This makes it incumbent on the seminary study program to include this aspect of the care that should be given to co-workers.

The seminary could be taken for the shepherd that nurses the young ones so that they in turn will take over the nursing in future in their parishes. We are here taking the seminary as an authority, personalizing the house of formation as the shepherd that is in charge of forming future shepherds. According to the pastoral formation program for St. Mary's Seminary & University, studies are taking the changing patterns of society into consideration. Candidates for the priesthood are schooled on how the parish functions, and given practical strategies on how to fulfill pastoral obligations. They are made to understand and appreciate the dynamics of prayer and prophecy. In this way the expected outcomes of the program will be reached with good results.[168] This is certainly conceived in the line of Pope John Paul II's exhortation on the gift of the priesthood in the church. He says, among other things, that the seminary will be a formation house in which the seminarians will be schooled in the

---

[167] Bernard Cooke, *Power and the Spirit of God: Toward an Experience-Based Pneumatology* (Oxford: Oxford University, 2004), 55.

[168] This is taken from private material on the Pastoral Formation Program of the seminary, with focus on leadership development for the next generation. This has been used with the permission of the director of Pastoral formation, Fr. David Couturier.

EVANGELIZATION IN CAMEROON: MAURICE MEI AKWA
Sight and Blindness in God's Revelation in Jesus Christ

Gospels and taught how to follow Christ.[169] The following image reflects that of the good shepherd who goes ahead of the sheep and the sheep follow after him. The seminary thus teaches the candidates to prepare for a future with ups and downs.

If there are still any seminaries in which formation is almost still exclusively academic, with the spiritual, interpersonal, and evangelical dimensions neglected, the results could be very tragic. The candidates will not have learned to build a relationship with Jesus and with one other, practicing what is taught. If the training is not given well or received well, what Fr. Couturier tried to discourage in January 2006 will continue lingering around the ministry of young or future pastors. He said: "We pull back so often in our lives and leave our brothers and sisters to face enormous pain alone. We're too busy to get involved, and remain so stressed out to become engaged. We find reason and excuses to pull back just enough to make it look like a good spiritual strategy. But, our God doesn't pull back. God's love is ecstatic. The God who lives in unapproachable light descends and enters our human condition."[170]

There are difficulties that will be encountered in the course of training. There will be temptations to quit or to be discouraged, but Jesus reassures the candidates in difficulty that he has conquered the world and so they should not be afraid. It is our wish that seminaries will set the pace for competent workers who will shepherd the flock of the Lord without fear or hesitation. This permits us to progress with how the good shepherd graced the Camcroonian land and how he affected the flock in that mission territory.

---

[169] John Paul II, *Pastores Dabo Vobis: On the Formation of Priests in the Circumstances of the Present Day* (Washington, D.C.: United States Conference of Catholic Bishops, 2002), 114.

[170] This is part of an unpublished sermon preached on January 27, 2006 entitled: *What Were You Thinking*.

CHAPTER FOUR

THE CASE OF CAMEROON IN AFRICA

Cameroon is a central African state on the Gulf of Guinea that begins the west coast of Africa. Its neighbors are Nigeria, Chad, Central African Republic, the Republic of Congo, Equatorial Guinea and Gabon. Compared to the US it is twice the size of Oregon.

171

---

[171] This compressed map of Cameroon shows the names of the ten provincial capitals highlighted in black ink.

Cameroon covers about 181,251 square miles, with a population of close to 19 million and a life expectancy of about 55.[172] Christianity is the religion of about 50% of the population, while Islam is practiced by 20% and traditional religions by 30%. These statistics show that Cameroon is still a missionary territory, in need of shepherds to seek out and convert those who have not yet heard the message into the fold.

In 1990 Cameroon celebrated one hundred years of evangelization, following the creation of the apostolic prefecture of Cameroon and the arrival of the first German missionaries in 1890. This prefecture was entrusted to the Pallotine Fathers as chief evangelizers of the territory, at the time a German colony.[173] The arrival of these missionaries was preceded by the baptism of the first Cameroonian, Kuo A. Mbangue on January 6, 1889 in Munich, Germany. He was serving as a bakery assistant in the Benedictine Monastery of St. Ottile.[174] The coincidence is that the missionaries first landed in his native homeland of Douala on October 25, 1890 and soon after, mission stations began to germinate as mushrooms in rapid succession.[175] How did this affect the lives of the local population?

The Light brought by Evangelization

In Cameroon, as in other areas of Africa, Christianity had a laborious birth. The local people and some local chiefs resisted

---

[172] The life expectancy of 55 is the recent official estimate. There are still rural areas where life expectancy remains about 45 for men and 41 for women.

[173] Cornelius F. Esua, *The Catholic Church in Cameroon 100 Years of Evangelization: 1890 Album of the Centenary 1990* (Yaoundé: The Cameroon National Episcopal Conference, 1990), 39.

[174] Ibid.

[175] Before the First World War began, after which the Germans were defeated and driven from their territories in Africa, there were 23 missions served by 34 priests, 36 brothers and 29 sisters.

EVANGELIZATION IN CAMEROON: MAURICE MEI AKWA
Sight and Blindness in God's Revelation in Jesus Christ

the establishment of the new religion that minimized their gods. When the missionaries persisted in asking for land, with the few early converts as their intermediaries, they were often given land in the evil forests, where the wicked spirits were known to dwell. It was here that those who died with deadly diseases such as leprosy were buried. Great fetishes were dumped here too when they passed away. So this was a place thought to be filled with sinister forces and powers of darkness. It was in the hope that the missionaries and their followers would be consumed by the spirits of the forest and thus be forgotten that they were assigned those forests for their settlement.[176] When the missionaries and the converts stayed there for months and nothing happened, other natives started coming in hesitantly or out of curiosity, to see what was going on. The missionaries had taken time to train some local interpreters so as to make the message they were bringing heard and understood.[177]

Little huts (tents) were built from local architecture to be the first churches. Then health posts were erected to cater for the health of the local population, with malaria, a number-one tropical killer disease, being the first target of the health workers who accompanied the missionaries inland.[178] Then schools were created to start forming the natives and teaching them how to read and write. This was a major breakthrough, although the first people to go close to the missionaries and to benefit from their services were mostly the outcasts of the local communities, and women. Outcasts were those who either had their property confiscated by the local chiefs in payment for a crime committed, those who had illness that the community regarded as unclean or

---

[176] Chinua Achebe, *Things Fall Apart* (New York: Anchor Books, 1994), 148.
[177] Ibid., 143.
[178] It should be noted that the German missionaries followed German colonial policies and were part of the colonial strategy. They therefore progressed in land with the permission of the local administrators and under their guidance and protection.

some who had committed felonies and had been exiled together with their families.

The first converts, therefore, knew what it meant to receive God's mercy and clemency. Young boys who went to school were either those who were heady at home or those that were lazy in the farms. These later on grew to be the light for the others when they were able to speak the white man's language and read and interpret his books. It is the ability to read the white man's book and interpret his language that attracted other families to send their children to school. These are those who would later on enter politics and join the local administration and thus become leaders of the new governments when Africa would fight for her independence from colonial masters.[179]

Making someone know what otherwise would not have been known is making that person see what otherwise would not have been seen. It is bringing light where there is darkness. It is bringing life where there was seemingly death. The coming of the missionaries to Cameroon in 1890 could be said to be a time of coming to light of the local population, the light of the gospel. From the coasts of Douala they traveled inland to create missions everywhere. They made the converts understand that they were the children of God, but also brothers and sisters, one of another. They were to uphold the faith under all circumstances, in good and bad weather. Twenty-five years later, at the end of the First World War, the German missionaries started leaving Cameroon. Missions were abandoned to themselves. Thank God that the missionaries had taken time to train catechists and assigned some of them to enclave areas.

---

[179] Anthony Ndi, *National Integration & Nation Building in Cameroon, the Golden Age of Southern (West) Cameroon 1946-1972: Impact of Christianity* (Bamenda: Maple Fair Services, 2005), 6.

It is these men who kept the community together and often traveled long distances, as far as to Nigeria or Equatorial Guinea to look for priests during feasts like Easter and Christmas. One of the priests who traveled from Nigeria, Mgr. Shanahan, described a four-month trek through Cameroon as the longest in his priestly ministry and the most interesting. At one station, a group of four men who had traveled four days on foot to come meet him brought a list of the sins of the Christians of their mission who could not make it to where he was and asked for the man of God's absolution.[180] These were people who were anxious to live in the light.

We said above that the missionaries built schools and hospitals. These became the principal education and health institutions of the country. Most-top ranking officers in the civil and military services in Cameroon were educated by missionaries. They were, therefore, expected to be influenced by their religious upbringing in their service to the nation and to its people. The light brought by the missionaries, therefore, helped in opening and exposing the people of Cameroon to the rest of the world.

We could compare the resistance put up by some chiefs and their local population to the religious leaders who resisted the light brought by Jesus. They thought they knew God but refused to recognize the signs of his dwelling among them in Jesus. The man born blind represents those underprivileged Africans who found refuge under the protection of the missionaries and became the first Christians. They knew what it meant to be separated from one's kindred, but they also tasted and felt how good it is to

---

[180] Martin Z. Njeuma, *A Pilgrimage of Faith: History of Buea Diocese* (Buea: Catholic Information Services, 2000), 29-30.

live under the protection of a shepherd.[181] Light means nothing to the one who is blind but when such a person is given back his sight, light becomes obvious. Christianity meant nothing to the Africans before they were evangelized, but now that the light of the Gospel has touched their land they know how good it is to have it.

Paul was angry with and saddened by the fact that the Galatians easily gave in to the influences of those who obliged them to live according to the Jewish law. He showed them that law reveals sin just as faith reveals righteousness. It is therefore their faith that justified them before God. They were not to begin such a beautiful life in the Spirit and end up with the flesh.[182] The coming of the missionaries therefore revealed the light to Africans in general and Cameroonians in particular. They have now become sheep to be taken care of. In the story of the good shepherd, we compare them to the other sheep that were not in the fold but that needed to be led and taken care of as well.[183] How are the sheep in Cameroon, therefore, taken care of?

Care of the Sheep and the Need for Good Shepherds

When the German Pallotine and Sacred Heart Fathers departed in 1918, there was a need more than ever for shepherds, spiritual leaders for the newfound communities. Their faith needed to be upheld so that it did not evaporate. November 1920 saw the arrival of St. Joseph Mill Hill missionaries in the West and the Holy Ghost and Oblate of Mary Immaculate Fathers in the Eastern part of Cameroon. They were later joined by the Sacred Heart Fathers. There came a mixture of English, Dutch

---

[181] Michael Willet Newheart, *Word and Soul: A Psychological, Literary, and Cultural Reading of the Fourth Gospel* (Collegeville: The Liturgical, 2001), 81.
[182] Galatians 3:1-14.
[183] John 10:16.

EVANGELIZATION IN CAMEROON: MAURICE MEI AKWA
Sight and Blindness in God's Revelation in Jesus Christ

and French missionaries, since Cameroon had been given as a trustee territory to Britain and France after the First World War.[184] The missionaries were of mixed nationalities. This new group of missionaries took the church through to the time of independence of Cameroon from former colonies,[185] making it possible for the Church in Cameroon to easily accommodate and get adapted to the reforms brought about by the Second Vatican Council, since it was going through reforms itself.

Christianity became the dominant religion in Cameroon after independence, and the Catholic Church emerged as the champion of the Christian course. The church moved from vicariates to seven dioceses. By the time the centenary celebrations took place there were nineteen dioceses. Lots of churches had been planted and bells rang everywhere to announce the good news. Black priests were increasing in their numbers, thus replacing the white missionaries who were gradually returning home.[186] Today there are twenty-three dioceses with four in the process of being created. This is the result that is obtained when the sheep are well cared for, well fed and well-protected. This was not without difficulties. Just as Jesus the good shepherd was accused of irregularities, so too was the church with its bishops.[187]

At independence, there were factions that were not satisfied with the way the government was set up and became a pressure opposition group to the new independent regime. When its demands were not met, it went underground and practiced guerilla fighting, commonly known in Cameroon as the 'Maqi.'

---

[184] Esua, *The Catholic Church in Cameroon*, 129.

[185] It should be noted that after the First World War, Cameroon was partitioned as a Trustee territory to England and France. The English took West Cameroon and the French took East Cameroon. That is why Cameroon has English and French as its official languages.

[186] Njeuma, *A Pilgrimage of Faith*, 83.

[187] John 9:24.

EVANGELIZATION IN CAMEROON: MAURICE MEI AKWA
Sight and Blindness in God's Revelation in Jesus Christ

A bishop was indicted and accused of collaborating with the rebels because he tried to negotiate and make them come out from underground.[188] Even Catholic Christians in government were made to testify that this was so, to the point where the Minister of Justice, a Catholic Christian himself, got involved. The bishop was exiled to Canada after illegal detention and being condemned by a makeshift tribunal to die by firing squad. The real reason behind the persecution was basically the fact that the Muslim president was convinced that there was a conspiracy within the Catholic hierarchy to overthrow him and install either a Catholic or another Christian leader as president.[189]

This did not deter the church leadership from playing its role as shepherd of the flock entrusted to it. The bishops in conference became the eyes and ears of the people, Christian and non-Christian alike, to the point where their opinion was always anxiously awaited whenever there was a crisis. Indeed the sheep recognized the voices of their shepherds as they strived to act according to the instructions of the church. The church continued to be the source of truth for them.[190] It is in this light that the bishops wrote pastoral letters to all Catholic priests, Christians and people of good will on the economic crises that hit the nation, on the value of life, marriage and contraception, elections, catholic schools and the means of mass communication.

---

[188] Bishop Albert Ndongmo was a no nonsense bishop who did everything to make his diocese exemplary even in the days when Cameroon was still struggling to get to its feet after independence. Since the guerilla activities were within his diocesan territorial boundaries, he felt it imperative on him to negotiate and end their strife so that their activities do not slow down the development of his area. Some people felt that he was too advanced for his time. He died abroad but his remains were brought back for burial in his diocese where he had long been replaced.

[189] Ndi, *The Golden Age of Southern (West) Cameroon*, 109.

[190] Joseph Cardinal Ratzinger, *Values in a Time of Upheaval. Translated by Brian McNeil* (New York: Crossroad, 2006), 55.

Some bishops were threatened anonymously, others openly, but they never gave up because the shepherd does not run away from the sheep when there is a threat. Instead, he faces the danger and protects or shields his sheep from being harmed. The bishops have stood the test of time and have seen the church grow from strength to strength.

191

In order that the sheep be well fed, many parishes were opened, and catechists trained to take care of the missions where the priest was not resident.[192] Priests stay in communities of two or three priests per parish to permit them to eat and pray together and not feel lonely and look at their work as burdensome.

---

[191] Although the dog in this picture is harmless, imagine it to be a wolf trying to attack the sheep. The shepherd stands there with his stick, his only weapon, ready to avert the danger.

[192] Parishes are made in such a way that each parish has several outstations or smaller missions in a radius of about 12.000 sq. miles or more. Each of these has a resident catechist who takes care of the spiritual needs of the faithful and prepares them for the monthly visit of the priest.

In 1985 Pope John Paul II showed his zeal for the care of the sheep as the chief shepherd of the church by paying a maiden visit to Cameroon. In the-five day visit that lasted from August 10-14, the Pope went to the four cities that were seats to the four Archdioceses in the country: Garoua, Douala, Bamenda and Yaoundé. Then he met with leaders of other religions and with the Christian intellectuals. It was a boost to the faith because after his visit there were many conversions to the Catholic faith. Christians made pilgrimages on foot for over 150 miles to come welcome him in every province. To show how close he was to the sheep he even greeted the Christians in some local languages, adding that their happiness in seeing the successor of Peter, the chief shepherd in their land, should be a sign of their "total acceptance of the gospel of Christ."[193]

Ten years later, in August 1995, the Pope was in Cameroon again. This time he came to officially close the special assembly for Africa of the Synod of Bishops and to inaugurate the post-synodal Apostolic Exhortation. According to Thomas Meh Chu, this visit was a necessity for the local churches to find their true faces from their own cultures. For him this was officially opening the way for the inculturation of evangelization in Cameroon, a means of familiarizing the care of the sheep.[194] The Pope insisted that evangelization must be an urgent activity in all churches, insisting that shepherds must strive to be the voice of the voiceless at all times. This is all the more possible if in evangelization, all that degrades and destroys the person is denounced and combated. For the Pope, "the condemnation of evils and injustices is also part of the ministry of evangelization

---

[193] Paul Verdzekov, *The Pope in Cameroon: Homilies and Addresses* (Yaoundé: SOPECAM, 1986), 59-60.

[194] Thomas Meh Chu, "John Paul II and Cameroon: the Silent Guide" in *John Paul II and Africa*, ed. S. Okechukwu Mezu & Rose Ure Mezu (Baltimore: Black Academy, 2005), 56.

in the social field which is an aspect of the church's prophetic role."[195]

It should be noted that this synod was held at a time when human events in Africa seemed to be tempting Africans to discouragement and despair due to the absence of peace caused by political instability and fratricidal wars.[196] Cameroon was plagued by mismanagement of resources and political chaos caused by an unstable multiparty system of government where the ruling party had the tendency of assimilating other smaller parties for strength and majority rule. The people of Africa at the time felt as if they were left on the edge of the highway of humanity, sick, injured, disabled, marginalized and abandoned in various ways when they were in dire need of a Good Samaritan to come their way and rescue them. The Synod did this and the post-synodal exhortation brought back hope. The urgency of proclaiming the good news and the necessity of a more profound evangelization made the need also of good shepherds all the more real. Like the man born blind, Africa seemed to have been abandoned by the rest of the world, but, like Jesus, the church was bringing back hope to the population to show them that God did not abandon them.

The church in Cameroon is a vibrant church with a rise in vocations and priestly ordinations. Thanks to the dedication and devotion of bishops, church institutions have been maintained. Mission schools are still among the best, as well as the mission medical facilities that are preferred because of the love that accompanies the care given to patients. The good shepherd pays

---

[195] John Paul II, *Post-Synodal Apostolic Exhortation: Ecclesia in Africa* (Vatican City: Vatican Press, 1995), 75.

[196] The genocide had just taken place in Rwanda, and Burundi was suffering the effects. The rebels were closing in on Freetown in Sierra Leone and Angola too had its own share of the unrest. Liberia was having its own problems but helping rebels in neighboring Cote d'Ivoire.

attention to the sick and weak sheep, and this is just what the church is out to do or is doing in Cameroon. For the standard to be maintained and for continuity to be possible, the church needs to have good shepherds, intelligent and holy priests who will be a source of encouragement too to their faithful.[197] Since the state of the economy determines the success of many projects, we will now compare the economic situation of the church in Cameroon with the man born blind.

The Man Born Blind and the Economic Situation of the Church In Cameroon [198]

The blind man was in need of healing for the glory of God to be revealed to him. He was born that way,[199] just as the missionaries met Africa as a poor community. The man was anxious after his healing to know who the Son of Man was, just as the Africans are anxious to live the word of God even in their poverty. In fact they live it happily though the church seems to live from hand to mouth daily. It is a poor church yet, it is incumbent at times on the pastor, it is his task, to make Christ felt and try to bring meaningful development. It is said that wherever the missionaries passed, development followed. This came in the form of schools, hospitals and market places that were built with financial assistance from the home missions or relatives and benefactors.

The man born blind had relied on his parents and the generosity of others to survive daily. There were certainly no schools to make him useful and at times self-reliant like the schools for the blind help make the blind today more useful to

---

[197] John Paul II, *Pastores Dabo Vobis,* 116.
[198] There are times when we will talk of Africa when we mean Cameroon. This is because what is true for Cameroon is true too for other African countries.
[199] John 9:1.

EVANGELIZATION IN CAMEROON: MAURICE MEI AKWA
Sight and Blindness in God's Revelation in Jesus Christ

themselves. That is also how the church has been in Africa, relying on the sympathy of the religious congregations that evangelized it, the friends of those missionaries and other churches of good will. They do this willingly like the shepherd who feeds his sheep and knows how to fulfill its need. Because of the economic state of the country and its people, and because the priests try to live a normal life, judiciously managing the bit they receive or obtain from missionary activities, the Christians tend to turn to them in times of difficulty. Priests are mistakenly taken to be rich when they do show generosity toward the needy. The church at times, therefore, is not only responsible for the spiritual wellbeing of the faithful, but also for their material wellbeing.[200]

The church cannot do otherwise than be involved in material development as well, since working for God's people entails knowing and serving them in their needs. In this way they will be led to know the One True God and be at his service. Bishop Awa even went as far as saying it is through this material satisfaction of the faithful that he came to know his sheep and maybe was known by them as well.[201]

There is an example of this in the letter to the Philippians where Paul thanks them for their solidarity in sending Epaphroditus to bring him provisions.[202] Although it is not the evangelizer helping the evangelized, it does bring out the importance of the one who has more helping the one who has little or nothing. Sent to bring gifts to Paul, Epaphroditus became himself a gift to Paul, as the things we do can have far-reaching consequences unknown or unimaginable to us. He became a

---

[200] Paul Verdzekov, *The Passing Away of a Great Missionary: Bishop Jules Peeters, MHM 1913-2002* (Bamenda: Copy Printing Technology, 2002), 23.
[201] Andrew Nkea, *Ut Cognoscant Te: the Life and Works of His Lordship Bishop Pius Suh Awa on the Occasion of his Episcopal Silver Jubilee* (Douala: Editions Universelles, 1996), 56-57.
[202] Philippians 2:25-30.

brother to Paul, a co-worker and co-soldier as he ministered to Paul's needs (2:25), even to the point of risking his own life in ill health for his friend and coming close to death (2:26).[203] After all, Jesus has shown that the shepherd is no good unless he is ready to risk his life for the sheep, not giving up in time of danger.[204]

The man born blind was tormented by the Pharisees because of his underprivileged status, as he was presumed to be born in sin. The church in Cameroon suffers this torment at times when the rich donors feel they could dictate the course of evangelization, or expect the church to close its eyes on their irregularities. Even in its poverty, the church is supposed to be the light at all times. It has to stand for the truth in time and out of time, and continue to teach it whether it is accepted or not, though, as Paul told Timothy, always with the aim of instructing.[205]

Just as poverty and being underprivileged did not discourage the man born blind from holding firm to the truth in Jesus, so too does the economic situation of the church in Cameroon not prevent it from holding firm to the truth of the gospel. It is very important for the church in Cameroon to remain this steadfast because Pope John Paul II described Cameroon as: "Africa in miniature: a melting-pot of numerous ethnic groups, rich in traditions, a crossroads of all the major religions of the African continent, at the meeting point of the French, and English-speaking worlds, with a remarkable demographic expansion and

---

[203] Michael Gorman, *Apostle of the Crucified Lord: A Theological Introduction to Paul & His Letters* (Grand Rapids: William B. Eerdmans, 2004), 440.
[204] John 10:12.
[205] 2 Timothy 4:1-2.

EVANGELIZATION IN CAMEROON: MAURICE MEI AKWA
Sight and Blindness in God's Revelation in Jesus Christ

great numbers of youth. This country has also been described as an island of peace."[206]

Peace is very important for the people of Cameroon. This seems to be one of the most important gifts the light of the gospel brought to the Cameroonians. All the countries that surround Cameroon have had one or several civil wars, but Cameroon has remained stable in peace since its independence. It is true that the peace was uneasy at times, but peace has always reigned and dominated.

In some very traditional areas, converts resettled around the church premises where they could peacefully live according to the gospel. Here they led lifestyles unacceptable to their own home communities, free from traditional social controls. Christians developed communities renowned for monogamy, collective lifestyle and, above all, education of their children.[207]

As education is also a light that drives away the darkness of poverty and ignorance, the education brought by the schools of the missionaries is gradually taking the church towards self-reliance. The man born blind grew steadily in his knowledge of Jesus until he came to proclaim him as Lord. Thus the stage was set for evangelization and the final revelation about Jesus. He was to be accepted in faith or rejected through blindness.[208] The church in Cameroon, too, needs to grow steadily in the light of the gospel and out of its poverty. This will certainly depend on how the local clergy handles the situation.

---

[206] Verdzekov, *The Pope in Cameroon*, 10.
[207] Jacqueline de Vries, *Catholic Mission, Colonial Government and Indigenous Response in Kom (Cameroon)* (Leiden: African Studies Centre, 1998), 63.
[208] Barnabas Lindars, *Behind the Fourth Gospel: Studies in Creative Criticism* (London: SPCK, 1971), 69.

EVANGELIZATION IN CAMEROON: MAURICE MEI AKWA
Sight and Blindness in God's Revelation in Jesus Christ

Jesus the Good Shepherd and the Task of the Local Clergy

Most of the people of the northern and northwestern grass fields of Cameroon live in a pastoral society. Sheep, goats and cows are the most common of animals kept for cash farming. They are mostly reared in the family and are kept around the family house, in a special enclosure. Every morning the head of the family comes out to give them salt or take them out to graze. It is quite interesting to see the behavior of these animals. They quickly recognize the funny clicking sounds and stick pointing of the shepherd and come bustling around him. Then when they go out to the field they are easily kept together as long as the shepherd is with them. He stays with them in the heat and when there is no shelter, in the rain and cold. He becomes part of the cattle and can distinguish each of them by name.

Parents take delight in teaching their children how to rear cattle. In fact, when they are growing up, boys receive an animal every year from the fathers when they reach cattle-shepherding age, so that they grow up to be good shepherds and their little flock with which they grew up becomes their settlement flock. Many children of cattle-rearing families do not go to school, which accounts for the low rate of education in some parts of Cameroon. Some schools too have devised a means of helping children from cattle-rearing cultures not to miss their tradition by introducing the keeping of cattle for student assignments.[209] It is therefore not difficult for the people to understand the role of the shepherd or to regard the religious leaders as such.

Some families with many cattle hire shepherds to look after a portion or all of the flock. The shepherd was expected to look after the flock under his responsibility and provide for it in

_____
[209] Camara Laye, *The African Child* (London: Fontana Books, 1970), 67.

everyway possible: bringing it to green pastures, giving it salt, taking it to the stream to drink, and providing it with refuge and security, making sure the flock was not harmed. This meant that the shepherd had a big leadership role to play.

The good shepherd sees to it that the sheep leave the fold orderly and goes ahead of them as they move into grazing land. The priest is called upon to see to the spiritual wellbeing of his faithful and make sure they live upright lives. This is only possible if he teaches them true doctrine and is of exemplary character before them. Priests must not be indifferent to the sufferings and joy of their Christians and must will to know them and be known by them. This is because the chief shepherd knows his sheep and his sheep know him.[210] This makes them different from hirelings. The priests will be considered hirelings if they look at the ministry as a profession for which they must be paid. Since the hireling works for payment, he can abandon his job at any time and get another one anywhere. But one who belongs takes the enterprise as a personal task, the fulfillment of a duty. When the priest knows his people and they know him, "he fulfills in his own person the special relationship between God and his people."[211] He is the link between God and his people. The ministry of the priest is to "preach the kingdom of God and baptize those who respond to the call to repentance."[212]

The Pharisees who said they were children of Abraham and so were free from the 'irregularities' of Jesus were proved to be blind and in sin. The disciples are those who accepted Jesus, recognizing that he is the Son of God. His word abides in them

---

[210] Michael S. Rose, *Priest: Portrait of Ten Good Men Serving the Church Today* (Manchester: Sophia Institute, 2003), 74.
[211] Ridderbos, 361.
[212] Robert Brancatelli, "Discipleship and the Logic of Transformative Catechesis," in *The Spirit in the Church and the World*, ed. Bradford E. Hinze (New York: Orbis Books, 2003), 221.

and they must continue to abide in Jesus' love so that they will no longer be slaves to sin. The priest, who is a disciple of Jesus and guarantor of the spiritual welfare of the Christians, must be aware of his delicate role and do well to defend the sheep from the evil one, even to the point of putting his life at risk for them.[213]

Jesus was a cause of division because of the brilliance of his message and the conviction of the signs he worked. Some said he was possessed because of the barriers he brought down while others were attentive enough to know that a possessed man could not have the power to open the eyes of a man born blind. The pastor is light to those around him. Not all his faithful will see his mission clearly, and he will be misjudged on many occasions. He must, therefore, work conscientiously, so that his work will convince them. Wherever the apostle passes carrying out similar duties like Jesus, since he is another Christ, he will arouse murmurs of aversion or of love. Jesus did not retaliate when he was wrongly accused. Instead he showed by the way he lived and preached that he was of God. He was a source of reconciliation, that which makes peace possible. [214] This is also the task of the priest who must conform himself to the master as the sheep do to the shepherd. We find this a necessity since Jesus, who lays down his life for his sheep, is doing the will of the Father.[215]

The priest in Cameroon understands this role. In most areas where parishes have resident priests, he is the focal point of the society. He is at times the most educated, the best lodged, and the only one with a car. Christians and non-Christians regard him as a moral authority and can easily notice when he goes out of the norms of his profession. He is a public figure. He must, therefore, be very sensitive to the feelings of those who expect much from

---

[213] Mary L. Coloe, *God Dwells with Us: Temple Symbolism in the Fourth Gospel* (Collegeville: Liturgical, 2001), 195.
[214] Ratzinger, 119.
[215] Anthony Tyrrell Hanson, *The Prophetic Gospel: A Study of John and the Old Testament* (Edinburgh: T&T Clark, 1991), 142.

him, and not be a source of scandal. To be able to keep up the light that must radiate around the pastor, there needs to be good training, and a type of economic autonomy.

Need for Solid Formation

John 9:2-4 shows an interesting dialogue between Jesus and his disciples. The disciples are curious about something and want to get the answer from Jesus whom they know has all the answers.[216] The disciples' question echoes something they know already in general Jewish views, but they want Jesus to confirm this or clarify it. Jesus does and goes ahead to tell them that work must be done when there is light, which is while time permits. This could be taken to represent the situation of candidates for the priesthood, future shepherds of God's flock. The time for seminary training is a time when the disciple asks questions for the master to clarify, a time when the disciple lets himself be formed by the master according to his convictions so as to be better prepared for the task ahead to minister to people of their time with all the challenges involved.[217]

Daylight, the time for work to be done for the seminarian, is the period of formation. During this time he will take advantage of the presence of the chief shepherd in his formators: teachers, mentors, confessors and those parishes that welcome him for pastoral experience to make the best of his formation. Christ needs to be brought to the poor, and it is the task of the priest to make him felt. For this to be a reality, those who work as shepherds need to be well formed, both spiritually and intellectually. In Cameroon the formation consists of a year of spiritual formation in the spiritual center, three years of philosophy and four years of theology. There is a pastoral

---

[216] John 6:67-68.
[217] McCormick, *The Critical Calling,* 128.

experience year after the philosophy cycle that brings the total years for formation to nine. Anyone who goes through this patiently and successfully should be ready for the ministry.[218]

The world seems to be in moral crises. The crises make the sheep discouraged and they have to look to the shepherd for encouragement and answers to their questions.[219] The sheep belong to the master and they are his own. They hear his voice and recognize it because they have heard it several times. The door they pass through is not opened to the stranger, so the shepherd is recognized when he passes through the door.[220] The seminarian belongs to the one who called him, and as he said, "it is not you who chose me, but I chose you and appointed you to go and bear fruit that will remain."[221] When he goes through formal formation and successfully fulfills the conditions, his ordination becomes a passage through the door. The Seminary and diocesan authorities become collectively the doorkeeper who lets him into the fold of his ministry. There he will get used to the sheep that are his faithful and they will learn and know his voice so as to follow his teaching.

It is when the training has been this successful that the new pastor, the new shepherd, becomes a source of unity for the sheep. The pastor and his sheep will be so united because of his legitimate training that the presence of God will be felt in their

---

[218] Christian Tumi, Editor, *The Training of Priests for the Church in Cameroon* (Nkolbisson: C E C, 1984) 16.

[219] Alan Paton, *Cry the Beloved Country* (New York: Scribner, 1987), 68-69.

[220] Nicholas Cachia, *The Image of the Good Shepherd as a Source for the Spirituality of the Ministerial Priesthood* (Roma: Editrice Pontificia Universita Gregoriana, 1997), 141.

[221] John 15:16.

EVANGELIZATION IN CAMEROON: MAURICE MEI AKWA
Sight and Blindness in God's Revelation in Jesus Christ

midst.[222] Otherwise, it will not be possible. For the shepherd to be more efficient, he needs some autonomy.

b) The Need for Self-Reliance

Self-reliance as we wish to look at it is the art of depending on one's own abilities, resources or judgment. This includes both intellectual and material autonomy. The church as an institution needs this to be able to maintain its authority. This autonomy will be felt in the way the priests and other mission workers are financially assisted, and the standard of life they lead.

There has been rapid growth in the Cameroonian community. The population has grown from six million citizens in the 1970s to about eighteen million today. The number of Catholic Christians has almost doubled, and the local priests and religious men and women are fast replacing the European missionaries. Of the thirty bishops that the country counts in twenty-three dioceses, only six are European. More and more priests are being ordained to the local church, as there are over a thousand seminarians in the five major seminaries.[223] We know it is the Lord who has called and chosen all these workers in his vineyard, and he will sanctify them so that through them his work may expand to other parts of the globe.

The material situation of the priests in particular is always very difficult as the local population is very poor and is not able to assist their churches and make them autonomous. The church

---

[222] Wilhelm Thusing, *La Prière Sacerdotale de Jésus (Jean Chapitre 17)*, traduit de l'Allemand par Joseph Burckel et François Stoessel (Paris: Cerf, 1970), 44-45.

[223] The Archdiocese of Bertoua, for example ordained 7 priests from 1997 to 2001. But from 2002 to 2006 28 priests have been ordained, a significant rise in the number of shepherds.

and the faithful are looking for solutions which will permit the priests to consecrate themselves completely to the works of their sacerdotal ministry of which the sheep are so much in need.[224] This calls for a fruitful and fraternal collaboration between the priests born in Cameroon and expatriate priests, so as to benefit from their mutual exchange. The church in Cameroon had depended on so many contributions sent to it by the congregations and family members of the expatriate missionaries. Today, European churches are becoming empty and the help comes hesitantly or, in some cases, it does not come at all.

Another aspect is technology. When the missionaries came to Cameroon, they came with religious brothers who were technicians. They built their own houses and repaired their vehicles. Construction shops were opened as well as car repair services. Local brothers were not trained in this field in most places, and when the missionaries attained the limit of age, they went back, leaving the structures to fall. In dioceses where preparation was made, these structures still serve, but they are few.[225] That is why, for the sheep to be cared for well, the shepherd needs some form of autonomy. Since this is not possible given the situation the country and the continent are going through, we propose a form of collaboration with the church in Europe and America.

The Church in Africa, Europe and America – Collaboration and Exchange

We have now come to the stage for proposal. The following proposal is made in order to let the light of faith shine brightly for the sheep to be better cared for. The churches in Europe and America are very much advanced in material development and

---

[224] Verzdekov, *The Pope in Cameroon*, 128-129.
[225] Njeuma, 59.

are autonomous bodies in the way they run their institutions. It is our wish, therefore, that the collaboration and complimentarity which was lacking in the relationship between the Pharisees and Jesus be made manifest in this newfound relationship between Africa, Europe and America. According to the chief shepherd of the church, "Nobody knows everything, but together we know what is needful: faith forms a network of mutual dependence that is at the same time a network of mutual solidarity, of supporting oneself and being supported."[226]

We therefore propose assistance in the **financial field**. Here, through regular financial appeals, clergy could be permitted, with the permission of their bishops, to come to parishes in the United States or Europe to talk to the faithful about projects they wish to accomplish in their various parishes. This will move the individual Christians to contribute free anonymous donations to help such parishes. Through official letters from the bishops as well, help could be asked from some church organizations such as the Knights of Columbus, Catholic Charities and other movements.

In another light, the church in America could pair up in **partnership** with some parishes or dioceses in Cameroon to permit them to stay closer to the rest of the world. In this way they will help to build structures like hospitals, schools and some local churches. These are the essential structures that make up the various churches in Cameroon.[227] We do not want the church that has received the light of the gospel to fall back into the darkness of discouragement. That is why it is necessary for this hand to be extended to sister churches. Where the structures already exist,

---

[226] Pope Benedict XVI, *The Yes of Jesus Christ: Exercises in Faith, Hope, and Love* (New York: Crossroad, 1991), 27-28.
[227] Building and construction are relatively cheap in the missions as the Christians themselves provide labor and most of the material like sand and stones.

they could benefit from instruments such as scientific equipment for hospitals and workshops, and books for schools.[228]

We encourage the practice of **scholarships** that is being extended to various churches to send candidates for the priesthood to study in American institutions.[229] This opens up such candidates to the American and world perspective so that wherever they find themselves in the world they will not feel left out. It is also our wish that this training be opened up to **specialized vocations** in various fields like pastoral counseling, personnel management, financial management, medical assistance, insurance, school administration, and law and otherwise. This specialized training could help the church establish its own structures that would generate finance and in the long run make it materially autonomous. The formation, too, will make the shepherd spiritually and intellectually strong and confident enough not to abandon the sheep when he sees a wolf in the form of some difficulty. He will be ready to lay down his life for the sheep, having learnt the importance and necessity of this self-offering.

Very soon there may be a shortage of priests and mission workers in the church in Europe and America. When this happens, Africa would become a **missionary donor**. Then an exchange program could be established in which priests could come from Cameroon to the US for a number of years, to serve in local parishes and thus make the presence of the Master felt.

---

[228] A book drive was recently organized for the library of the major seminary in Bertoua Archdiocese in Cameroon. It was more than successful as many professors and friends of Bertoua donated a bit more than 2000 books. These are being shipped free to Cameroon, thanks to the efforts of Dr. Michael Gorman, Professor. This is a good sign of collaboration between St. Mary's Seminary and University and the Church in Cameroon.

[229] St. Mary's Seminary & University has had a tradition of training seminarians for the Archdiocese of Douala, Cameroon. This generosity was recently extended to the Archdiocese of Bertoua.

GENERAL CONCLUSION

We have tried to show the revelation of God in Jesus Christ through our exposition on sight and blindness with a focus on John 9:1-10:21. We showed sight as light and blindness as darkness and tried to bring out how Jesus the light is the good shepherd. He leads the way in virtuous living and shows what it means to care for the weak ones of the community. Sin is what prevents us from seeing clearly and doing what should be done, the way it should be done. When pride prevents the individual from seeing and accepting the truth, the blindness is even greater. The Messiahship of Jesus, and the blind and pitiful rejection of him by the Jewish leaders, and the response made to him in faith by those whose spiritual desires or sense of need caused them to listen to his gracious message, bring out the notion of light in contrast to darkness. Those who accept him are in the light and have sight, while those who reject him are in the darkness and are blind.

This is what we brought out in the spiritual journey of the man born blind through which the glory of God is manifested in Jesus Christ. He progressively comes to full sight, while the Pharisees who claim to see ironically become blind, because they refuse to accept that Jesus is the Messiah they had been waiting for. Because they claim to see and yet show how ignorant they are, Jesus proclaims them sinners (John 9:41), the same accusation they levy on Jesus and the man he has healed. Jesus proves to them that "he came to unveil lies, illusions and hypocrisy, [and] to give witness to the truth, to lead people to the God of compassion and forgiveness."[230] He does this by showing his role as a good shepherd in contrast to the Jews who came

---

[230] Jean Vanier, *Drawn to the Mystery of Jesus through the Gospel of John* (New York: Paulist, 2004), 10.

before him. They are bad shepherds, acting as hirelings with no care for the sick and weak sheep (such as the man born blind), just as the kings and priests of old acted as portrayed in Ezekiel 34. Through his discussion about the good shepherd, Jesus brings to light the holiness and love of God, whose will he is obeying. He thus shows himself as the Messiah whose voice the sheep know and follow faithfully.

When leadership is executed in the light of the good shepherd, be it in church, in the civil society or in formation houses, it is bound to succeed. That is why we have proposed a systematic, good and solid formation in our seminaries, as exemplified in the formation carried out in St. Mary's Seminary & University, with the recent update on pastoral formation and management.

The coming of the gospel to Cameroon, in particular, and Africa, in general, has also been seen as the coming of light to enlighten those other sheep that the good shepherd said were going to be brought to the fold. Africa in its vast variety and rich culture has embraced the Christian faith and is intensifying its love for the word and the Lord.

We compared Africa to the man born blind. For no fault of his, he was born blind so that God's glory might be manifested, since pain can be permitted by God to make his glory realized. Africa too is poor and, therefore, stands out as a weak sheep in need of guidance. Good shepherds are needed for the care of the vibrant church.

We therefore proposed the material and financial help of America and Europe for the construction of some local infrastructure and the training of some local clergy in specialized fields.[231] This could become that means through which the glory of God will be manifested. The seminarians and priests need solid formation so that the church will be assured of the continuous burning of the light of faith among its people in the bearers of the word through their preaching and example of living.

This has been a scientific work in which we tried to show Jesus as the light, knowing that the theme of light is one of the dominant themes of the Gospel of John. With the support of other sources we tried to show that the world needs light, the light of Christ, for its difficulties to be overcome. It is our wish that all people will come to know him and accept him so that there will one day be one flock and one shepherd.

---

[231] We noted above that there are scholarships already existing in St. Mary's Seminary & University for some African dioceses.

BIBLIOGRAPHY

Achebe, Chinua. *Things Fall Apart*. New York: Anchor Books, 1994.

Anderson, Paul N. *The Christology of the Fourth Gospel: Its Unity and Disunity in the Light of John 6*. Valley Forge, Pennsylvania: Trinity International, 1997.

Achtemeier, Elizabeth. *The Old Testament and the Proclamation of the Gospel*. Philadelphia: Westminster, 1952.

Ashton, John. *Studying John: Approaches to the Fourth Gospel*. Oxford: Clarendon, 1994.

_____ *Understanding the Fourth Gospel*. Oxford: Clarendon, 1993.

Asiedu-Peprah, Martin. *Johannine Sabbath Conflicts as Juridical Controversy*. Tubingen: Mohr Siebeck, 2001.

Ball, David M. *'I Am' in John's Gospel: Literary Function, Background and Theological Implications*. Sheffield: Sheffield, 1996.

Bartlett, David L. "The First Letter of Peter: Introduction, Commentary, and Reflections." In *The New Interpreter's Bible*, ed., Leander E. Keck et al., Vol. 12, 227-319. Nashville: Abingdon, 1994-2004.

Bright, Laurence. *Scripture Discussion Commentary*. Chicago: Acta Foundation, 1972.

Borg, Marcus J. and N.T. Wright. *The Meaning of Jesus: Two Visions*. San Francisco: Harper Collins, 1998.

Brancatelli, Robert. "Discipleship and the Logic of Transformative Catechesis." In *The Spirit in the Church and the World*, ed. Bradford E. Hinze. 219-238. New York: Orbis, 2003.

Brown, Raymond E. *An Introduction to the Gospel of John*. Ed. Francis J. Moloney. New York: Doubleday, 2003.

_____ *An Introduction to the New Testament*. New York: Doubleday, 1997.

91

_____ *The Community of the Beloved Disciple: The Life, Loves and Hates of an individual Church in the New Testament Times.* New York: Paulist, 1979.

_____ *The Gospel and Epistles of John: A Concise Commentary.* Collegeville, Minnesota: Liturgical, 1988.

Byrne, Brendan. *The Hospitality of God: A Reading of Luke's Gospel.* Collegeville: Liturgical, 2000.

Cachia, Nicholas. *The Image of the Good Shepherd as a Source for the Spirituality of the Ministerial Priesthood.* Roma: Editrice Pontificia Universita Gregoriana, 1997.

Charlesworth, James H. *John and the Dead Sea Scrolls.* New York: Crossroads, 1990.

Chu, Thomas M. "John Paul II and Cameroon: the Silent Guide" in *John Paul II and Africa,* Edited by S. Okechukwu Mezu & Rose Ure Mezu. 52-57. Baltimore Black Academy, 2005.

Coleridge, Mark. *The birth of the Lukan Narrative: Narrative as Christology in Luke 1-2.* Sheffield: Sheffield, 1993.

Coloe, Mary L. *God Dwells within Us: Temple Symbolism in the Fourth Gospel.* Collegeville: Liturgical, 2001.

Cooke, Bernard. *The Power and the Spirit of God: Toward an Experience-Based Pneumatology.* Oxford: Oxford University, 2004.

Craddock, Fred B. "The Letter to the Hebrews: Introduction, Commentary, and Reflections." In *The New Interpreter's Bible,* ed., Leander E. Keck et al., Vol. 12, 1-173. Nashville: Abingdon, 1994.

Crenshaw, James L. *Old Testament Wisdom: An Introduction.* Louisville: Westminster John Knox, 1998.

Cross, F.L. and E.A. Livingstone. *The Oxford Dictionary of the Christian Church.* London: Oxford University, 1974.

Culpepper, Alan R. *Anatomy of the Fourth Gospel: A Study in Literary Design.* Philadelphia: Fortress, 1983.

_____ *The Gospel and Letters of John.* Nashville: Abingdon, 1998.

Dauphinais, Michael and Matthew L. *Reading John with St. Thomas Aquinas: Theological Exegesis and Speculative Theology*. Washington, D.C.: Catholic University of America, 2005.

Davidson, Robert. *The Vitality of Worship: A commentary on the Book of Psalms*. Edinburgh: Handsel, 1998.

Duke, Paul D. *Irony in the Fourth Gospel*. Atlanta: John Knox, 1985.

Dumm, Demetrius R. *A Mystical Portrait of Jesus: New Perspectives on John's Gospel*. Collegeville, Minnesota: Liturgical, 2001.

Esua, Cornelius F. *The Catholic Church in Cameroon 100 Years of Evangelization: 1890 Album of the Centenary 1990*. Yaoundé: The Cameroon National Episcopal Conference, 1990.

Flannery, Austin. *Vatican Council II: The Conciliar and Post Conciliar Documents*. New York: Costello, 1996.

Gaillardetz, Richard R. *By What Authority? A Primer on Scripture, the Magisterium, and the Sense of the Faithful*. Collegeville: Liturgical, 2003.

Garrigou-Lagrange, Reginald. *The Priest in Union with Christ*. Rockford: Tan Books, 2002.

Gorman, Michael. *Apostle of the Crucified Lord: A Theological Introduction to Paul & His Letters*. Grand Rapids: William B. Eerdmans, 2004.

Gowan, Donald E. *Theology of the Prophetic Books: The Death & Resurrection of Israel* Louisville: Westminster John Knox, 1989.

Green, Joel B. *The Theology of Luke*. Cambridge: Cambridge University, 2004.

Haenchen, Ernst. *John 2: A Commentary on the Gospel of John Chapters 7-21*. Philadelphia: Fortress, 1984.

Hairing, Bernard. *Free and Faithful in Christ: Moral Theology for Clergy and Laity. Volume 1: General Moral Theology*. New York: Seabury, 1978.

EVANGELIZATION IN CAMEROON: MAURICE MEI AKWA
Sight and Blindness in God's Revelation in Jesus Christ

Hakola, Raimo. *Identity Matters: John, the Jews and Jewishness*. Boston: Brill, 2005.

Hanson, Paul D. *Isaiah 40-66: Interpretation. A Bible Commentary for Teaching and   Preaching*. Louisville: John Knox, 1995.

Hanson, Anthony T. *The Prophetic Gospel: A Study of John and the Old Testament* Edinburgh: T&T Clark, 1991.

Jan, de Jonge Henk. "The Jews in the Gospel of John." *In Anti-Judaism and the Fourth Gospel*, ed. R. Bieringer, D. Pollefeyt, and F. Vandecasteele-Vanneuville. 121-140. Louis: Westminster John Knox, 2001.

John Paul II. *Letter to my Brother Priests, 1979-2001*, ed. James Socias. Princeton: Scepter, 2001.

_____ *Pastores Dabo Vobis: On the Formation of Priests in the Circumstances of the Present Day*. Washington D.C.: The United States Conference of Catholic Bishops, 2002.

_____ *Post-Synodal Apostolic Exhortation: Ecclesia in Africa*. Vatican City: Vatican Press, 1995.

Keener, Craig S. *The Gospel of John: A Commentary. Volume 1*. Peabody: Hendrickson, 2003.

Kelly, Anthony J. and Moloney J. Francis. *Experiencing God in the Gospel of John*. New York: Paulist, 2003.

Kieffer, René. *Le Monde Symbolique de Saint Jean*. Latour-Maubourg: Cerf, 1989.

Kim, Hyun Chul Paul. *Ambiguity, Tension, and Multiplicity in Deutero- Isaiah*. New York: Peter Lang, 2003.

Kirk, Albert and Obach E. Robert. *A Commentary on The Gospel of John*. New York: Paulist, 1981.

Klein, Ralph W. *Ezekiel: The Prophet and his Message*. Columbia: University of South Carolina, 1988,

Koester, Craig R. *Symbolism in the Fourth Gospel. Meaning, Mystery, Community*. Second Edition. Minneapolis: Fortress, 2003.

Kostenberger, Andreas J. *Encountering John: The Gospel in Historical, Literary, and Theological Perspective*. Grand Rapids: Baker, 1999.

_____ "The Death of Jesus and the Human Condition: Exploring the Theology of John's Gospel." In *Life in Abundance: Studies of John's Gospel in Tribute to Raymond E. Brown*, ed. John R. Donahue. 141-157. Collegeville: Liturgical, 2005.

Kysar, Robert. *John's Story of Jesus*. Philadelphia: Fortress, 1984.

Landau, I. Sidney. *The New Webster's Concise Dictionary of the English Language: Encyclopedic Edition*. Naples, Florida: Trident International, 2003.

Laye, Camara. *The African Child*. London: Fontana, 1970.

Lee, Dorothy. *Flesh and Glory: Symbolism, Gender and Theology in the Gospel of John.* New York: Crossroad, 2002.

Lincoln, Andrew T. *Black's New Testament Commentaries: The Gospel According to Saint John*, ed. Morna D. Hooker. New York: Continuum, 2005.

Lindars, Barnabas. *Behind the Fourth Gospel: Studies in Creative Criticism*. London: SPCK, 1971.

Malina, Bruce J. and Rohrbaugh L. Richard. *Social Science Commentary on the Gospel of John*. Minneapolis: Fortress, 1998.

Marrow, Stanley B. *The Gospel of John: A reading*. New York: Paulist, 1995.

Martyn, Louis J. *History and Theology in the Fourth Gospel*. Third Edition. Louisville: Westminster John Knox, 2003.

Matson, Mark A. *John*. Louisville: Westminster John Knox, 2002.

McCormick, Richard A. *The Critical calling: Reflections on the Moral Dilemmas Since Vatican II*. Washington, D.C. Georgetown University, 1989.

McPolin, James. *John*. Collegeville: Liturgical, 1993.

Moloney, Francis J. *Belief in the word. Reading the fourth Gospel: John 1-4*. Minneapolis: Fortress, 1993.

95

_____ *Signs and Shadows: Reading John 5-12.* Minneapolis: Fortress, 1996.

_____ *The Gospel of John: Text and Context.* Boston: Brill Academic   Publishers, 2005.

_____ *The Gospel of John. Sacra Pagina Series Volume 4.* Edited by Harrington J. Daniel. Collegeville, Minnesota: Liturgical, 1998.

Morris, Leon. *Jesus is the Christ: Studies in the Theology of John.* Michigan: William B. Eerdmans, 1989.

_____ *Reflections on the Gospel of John.* Peabody, Massachusetts: Hendrickson, 2000.

Ndi, Anthony. *National Integration & Nation Building in Cameroon, the Golden Age of Southern (West) Cameroon: Impact of Christianity.* Bamenda: Maple Fair Services, 2005.

Newbigin, Lesslie. *The Light has come: An exposition of the Fourth Gospel.* Grand Rapids: William B. Eerdmans, 1997.

Newheart, Michael W. *Word and Soul: A Psychological, Literary, and Cultural Reading of the Fourth Gospel.* Collegeville: Liturgical, 2001.

Nkea, Andrew. *Ut Cognoscant Te: The Life and Work of His Lordship Bishop Pius Suh Awa on the occasion of his Episcopal Silver Jubilee.* Douala: Universelles, 1996.

Odell, Margaret S. and Strong T. John. *The Book of Ezekiel, Theological and Anthropological Perspectives.* Atlanta: Society of Biblical Literature, 2000.

Orchard, Helen C. *Courting Betrayal: Jesus as Victim in the Gospel of John.* Sheffield: Sheffield Academic Press, 1998.

Paton, Alan. *Cry the Beloved Country.* New York: Scribner, 1987

Pazdan, Mary M. *The Son of Man: A Metaphor for Jesus in the Fourth Gospel.* Collegeville: Liturgical, 1991.

Petersen, Norman R. *The Gospel of John and the Sociology of Light: Language and Characterization in the Fourth Gospel.* Valley Forge, Pennsylvania: Trinity International, 1993.

Pope Benedict XVI. *The Yes of Christ: Exercises in Faith, Hope and Love*. New York: Crossroad, 1991.

Powell, Mark A. *Fortress Introduction to the Gospels*. Minneapolis: Fortress, 1998.

Ratzinger, Joseph C. *Values in a Time of Upheaval*. Translated by Brian McNeil. New York: Crossroad, 2006.

Rensberger, David. *Johannine Faith and Liberating Community*. Philadelphia: Westminster, 1988.

Rho, Chi. *Commentary on the Gospel According to John*. Adelaide: Lutheran, 1988.

Richardson, Ronald W. *Creating a Healthier Church: Family Systems Theory, Leadership, and Congregational Life*. Minneapolis: Fortress, 1996.

Ridderbos, Herman. *The Gospel According to John: A Theological Commentary*. Translated by John Vriend. Grand Rapids: William B. Eerdmans, 1997.

Ringe, Sharon H. *Wisdom's Friends: Community and Christology in the Fourth Gospel*. Louisville: Westminster John Knox, 1999.

Rose, Michael S. *Priest: Portrait of Ten Good Men Serving the Church Today*. Manchester: Sophia Institute, 2003.

Rosse, Gerard. *The Spirituality of Communion: A New Approach to the Johannine Writings*. New York: New City, 1998.

Schneiders, Sandra M. *Written that you may believe: Encountering Jesus in the Fourth Gospel*. New York: Crossroad, 2003.

Segovia, Fernando F. *"What is John?" Readers and Readings of the Fourth Gospel*. Atlanta: Scholars, 1996.

Senior, Donald. *The Gospel of Matthew*. Nashville: Abingdon Press, 1997.

Sinclair, G. Scott, *The Road and the Truth: Editing of John's Gospel*. Vallejo: BIBAL, 1994.

Smith, D. Moody, *John among the Gospels*, Second Edition. Columbia: University of South Carolina, 2003.

97

_____ *Johannine Christianity: Essays on its Setting, Sources, and Theology*. Columbia: University of South Carolina, 1989.

_____ "John." In *The HarperCollins Bible Commentary*, ed. Mays L. James. 956-986. San Francisco: HarperCollins, 1988.

_____ *New Testament Theology: The Theology of the Gospel of John*. Cambridge: Cambridge University, 1996.

Stibbe, Mark W. G. *John's Gospel*. New York: Routledge, 1994.

Stravinskas, Peter M. J. *Our Sunday Visitor's Catholic Encyclopedia*. Huntington: Our Sunday Visitor, 1994.

Talbert, Charles H. *Reading John: A Literary and Theological Commentary on the Fourth Gospel and the Johannine Epistles*. New York: Crossroad, 1994.

Taylor, Michael J, *A Companion to John: Readings in Johannine Theology (John's Gospel and Epistles)*. New York: Alba House, 1977.

Thurston, Bonnie B. *Preaching Mark*. Minneapolis: Fortress, 2002.

Thusing, Wilhelm. *La Prière Sacerdotale de Jésus (Jean Chapitre 17)*. Traduit de l'Allemand par Joseph Burckel et François Stoessel. Paris: Cerf, 1970.

Tumi, Christian. *The Training of Priests for the Church in Cameroon*. Nkolbisson: C. E. C., 1984.

Vanier, Jean. *Drawn into the Mystery of Jesus through the Gospel of John*. New York: Paulist, 2004.

Verdzekov, Paul. *The Passing away of a Great Missionary: Bishop Jules Peeters, MHM 1913-1002*. Bamenda: Copy Printing Technology, 2002.

_____ *The Pope in Cameroon: Homilies and Addresses*. Yaoundé: SOPECAM, 1986.

Vries, Jacqueline. *Catholic Mission, Colonial Government and Indigenous Response in Kom (Cameroon)*. Leiden: African Studies Centre, 1998.

EVANGELIZATION IN CAMEROON: MAURICE MEI AKWA
Sight and Blindness in God's Revelation in Jesus Christ

Welch, Robert H. *Church Administration: Creating Efficiency for Effective Ministry*. Nashville: Broadman & Holman, 2005.

Wijngaads, John. *The Gospel of John & Letters*. Wilmington: Michael Glazier, 1986.

www.ingramcontent.com/pod-product-compliance
Lightning Source LLC
Chambersburg PA
CBHW060358050426
42449CB00009B/1803